ITALIAN PICTURE DICTIONARY COLORING BOOK

Over 1500 Italian Words and Phrases
for Creative & Visual Learners of All Ages

Color and Learn

Lingo Mastery

ISBN: 978-1-951949-50-1

Free Book Reveals The 6 Step Blueprint That Took Students **From Language Learners To Fluent In 3 Months**

- **6 Unbelievable Hacks** that will accelerate your learning curve
- **Mind Training:** why memorizing vocabulary is easy
- **One Hack To Rule Them All:** This <u>secret nugget</u> will blow you away...

Head over to **LingoMastery.com/hacks** and claim your free book now!

CONTENTS

Introduction 1

BASICS OF THE ITALIAN LANGUAGE 2

EMOZIONI (Emotions) 22

LA FAMIGLIA (The Family) 24

RELAZIONI (Relationships) 26

VALORI (Values) 28

IL CORPO UMANO (The Human Body) 30

NEL CORPO UMANO (Inside the Human Body) 32

ANIMALI DOMESTICI (Pets) 34

LO ZOO (The Zoo) 36

UCCELLI (Birds) 38

QUIZ #1 40

RETTILI E ANFIBI (Reptiles and Amphibians) 42

INSETTI E ARACNIDI (Insects and Arachnids) 44

MAMMIFERI I (Mammals I) 46

MAMMIFERI II (Mammals II) 48

PESCI E MOLLUSCHI (Fish and Mollusks) 50

VESTITI I (Clothing I) 52

VESTITI II (Clothing II) 54

IL TEMPO (The Weather) 56

LE STAGIONI - PRIMAVERA (The Seasons – Spring) 58

LE STAGIONI - ESTATE (The Seasons – Summer) 60

QUIZ #2 62

LE STAGIONI – AUTUNNO (The Seasons – Fall/Autumn) 64

LE STAGIONI - INVERNO (The Seasons – Winter) 66

TEMPO (Time) 68

LA CASA (The House)..70

ELEMENTI DELLA CUCINA (Kitchen Items) 72

ELEMENTI DELLA CAMERA DA LETTO (Bedroom Items) 74

ELEMENTI DEL BAGNO (Bathroom Items)...76

ELEMENTI DEL SALOTTO (Living Room Items) 78

ELEMENTI DELLA SALA DA PRANZO (Dining Room Items) 80

QUIZ #3 82

IL GIARDINO (The Garden/The Backyard) 84

LA STANZA DEL BUCATO (The Laundry Room)...86

LA SCUOLA (The School/The University) 88

L'UFFICIO (The Office)..90

PROFESSIONI (Professions/Occupations)...92

MEZZI DI TRASPORTO (Means of Transport) 94

PAESAGGI (Landscapes) 96

SPORT I (Sports I)..98

SPORT II (Sports II) 100

IL GIORNO DI NATALE (Christmas Day) 102

QUIZ #4 104

STRUMENTI MUSICALI (Musical Instruments) 106

FRUTTA (Fruits) 108

VERDURE (Vegetables) 110

TECNOLOGIA (Technology)..112

SCIENZA (Science)...114

ASTRONOMIA (Astronomy) 116

GEOGRAFIA (Geography)...118

L'OSPEDALE (The Hospital) 120

LA FATTORIA (The Farm)...122

QUIZ #5 124

CIBO (Food) 126

PIATTI (Dishes)...128

FRUTTI DI MARE (Seafood) 130

FORME (Shapes) 132

IL SUPERMERCATO (The Supermarket) 134

MEDIA (Media) 136

LA FIERA/IL PARCO DIVERTIMENTI (The Fair/The Amusement Park) 138

EVENTI DI VITA (Life Events) 140

AGGETTIVI I (Adjectives I) 142

QUIZ #6 144

AGGETTIVI II (Adjectives II) 146

AVVERBI (Adverbs) 148

DIREZIONI (Directions) 150

IL RISTORANTE (The Restaurant) 152

IL CENTRO COMMERCIALE (The Mall) 154

VERBI I (Verbs I) 156

VERBI II (Verbs II) 158

COSTRUZIONI I (Construction I) 160

COSTRUZIONI II (Construction II) 162

QUIZ #7 164

PIANTE E ALBERI (Plants and Trees) 166

IL CARNEVALE (The Carnival) 168

L'OFFICINA (The Workshop) 170

IL NEGOZIO DI ALIMENTARI (The Grocery Store) 172

VIAGGI E VITA I (Travel and Living I) 174

VIAGGI E VITA II (Travel and Living II) 176

GIOCATTOLI (Toys) 178

LA FESTA DI COMPLEANNO (The Birthday Party) 180

CONTRARI (Opposites) 182

QUIZ #8 184

Conclusion 186

Answers 187

INTRODUCTION

The Italian Picture Dictionary Coloring Book is a fun vocabulary building tool with illustrations that you can color while learning. We will cover a wide range of topics, while giving you some useful suggestions to start talking like a local.

Learning a new language is always a challenge, but this is a fun and enjoyable way to practice your vocabulary, spelling and grammar!

Some people say that they are simply not good at languages, but that is not true. To learn a new language, all it takes is practice, practice, practice. And we are here to help you throughout this journey!

Buona fortuna, good luck!

BASICS OF THE ITALIAN LANGUAGE

I.   L'Alfabeto – The Alphabet

You might ask yourself why you should start with the alphabet, as it could seem like the kind of thing you would do in school. Actually, as Italian is a **phonetic** language, the pronunciation of a word is made up of the single sound of each letter.

This means that, once you learn how to read the Italian letters, you will be able to read sentences and texts right away. There are just a few combinations of letters that have a slightly different sound, but we will cover them as well.

In Italian schools, spelling exercises are not that common as, once you listen to a specific word, you already know how to write it because you immediately recognize all its letters.

The only thing that might be a little more difficult, especially for foreigners, is to recognize when there are **doubled** letters. Even if it is not a big issue when talking—as you can still understand the meaning of that word in a given context—it is quite important while writing, because sometimes a word can have a completely different meaning if you don't double a letter.

Examples:

- *pena* (punishment) vs *penna* (pen)

- *caro* (dear) vs *carro* (cart)

- *tori* (bulls) vs *torri* (towers)

How can you recognize when there is a doubled letter, then? Well, the sound of that letter will be longer and more pronounced. Of course, recognizing it will also get easier with time, as you gradually learn new words and how to write them.

The tables below provide information on the alphabet, the names and pronunciations of the individual letters, and a guide to the sounds they produce in words.

Letter	Letter name / Pronunciation		Pronunciation guide
a	a	ah	Like **a** in **father**
b	bi	be	Same as in English
c	ci	chi	Like **ch** in **chili**
d	di	de	Like the corresponding letter in the English alphabet
e	e	ai	Like **a** in **way** or **ai** in **fair**
f	effe	eh-feh	Same as in English (like the f in father)
g	gi	gi	Like **g** in **gym**
h	acca	ah-kah	Always silent
i	i	ee	Like **ee** in feet
j	i lunga	e loongah	Same pronunciation as the letter **g**
k	kappa	kah-ppah	Same as in English
l	elle	eh-lleh	Same as in English
m	emme	eh-mmeh	Same as in English
n	enne	eh-nneh	Same as in English
o	o	oh	Like the **o** sound in **opera**

p	*pi*	*pe*	Same as in English
q	*qu*	*koo*	Like the English **k** (always followed by u)
r	*erre*	*eh-rreh*	Like the English **r** but rolled
s	*esse*	*eh-sseh*	Same as in English
t	*ti*	*te*	Like **t** in **tee-shirt**
u	*u*	*oo*	Like the **oo** in **school**
v	*vu*	*voo*	Like the **v** in **vendor**
w	*doppia vu*	*doh-ppeah voo*	Same pronunciation as letter **v**
x	*ics*	*eks*	Same as in English
y	*ipsilon*	*epselon*	Same pronunciation as letter **i**
z	*zeta*	*seh-tah*	Pronounced as **dz**, similar to the English **zebra**

Please note that letters **j, k, w, x and y** are called "foreign letters" and do not belong to the Italian alphabet. We added them in the table above because they can be useful, for example, if you need to spell your name or other words in English. In fact, most words using those letters are English ones—examples: jeans, K-Way, yo-yo etc.

As mentioned before, you would read most of these letters in the same way you pronounce them while reading the alphabet. However, there are some combinations of letters that need to be read in a specific way. Please take a look at the table below and have fun while practicing!

Letter	Letter name / Pronunciation		Pronunciation guide
che	che	keh	Like ca in caption
chi	chi	kè	Like key
ca	ca	kah	Like ca in category
ce	ce	che	Like che in cheddar
ci	ci	chi	Like chi in chimney
co	co	koh	Like co in company
cu	cu	kuh	Like cou in couscous
sci	sci	she	Like she
ghe	ghe	geh	Like ge in get
ghi	ghi	gih	Like gi in gift
ga	ga	gah	Like ga in garage
ge	ge	geh	Like ge in generation
gi	gi	ge	Like gi in ginger
go	go	goh	Like go in got
gu	gu	guh	Like gu in guru
gl	gl	ll	Probably, the most difficult sound to pronounce. It is like the Spanish ll—you barely read the letter g. In English, it sounds like ly as in hardly

We know, it might seem that there are many exceptions, but if you take a closer look, you will notice that it is actually always the same rule applying to different letters.

Once you learn their pronunciation, you will be ready to start writing in Italian as well!

In case you're wondering what to do when you have a **diphthong**—which is the combination of two vowels—once again, Italian is easier than English. In Italian, you just have to pronounce those two vowels separately, as you would read them in the alphabet. They do not produce a different sound.

Examples:

- *camion* (truck) – Pronounced as *kah-me-ohn*

- *buono* (good) – Pronounced as *buh-oh-noh*

- *guanto* (glove) – Pronounced as *guh-ahn-toh*

One last important thing about reading Italian words: you <u>always</u> read the last letter as well.

II.   L'accento – The accent

The Italian accent can be either **tonic**—i.e., it falls on one of the syllables, always on a vowel—or **graphic**—i.e., it has to be written.

For the graphic accent, there are a couple of things you need to know:

- It is always on the <u>last</u> letter of the word.

- It can be <u>acute</u>—it points to the right! —or <u>grave</u> – it points to the left!

Let's see some examples in order to show you the difference in terms of pronunciation:

- Acute accent: *perché* (why/because) – The sound of the letter *e* is a closed one, and the word pronunciation is per-keh.

- Grave accent: *tè* (tea) – The sound of the letter *e* is an open one, like the sound of the first **te** in **template**.

Why is it so important to write the graphic accent when needed? Well, because if you do not write it, sometimes a word can take a completely different meaning.

Examples:

- *papà* (dad) vs *papa* (pope)

- *però* (but) vs *pero* (pear tree)

- *è* (he/she/it is) vs *e* (and)

III.   I verbi – The verbs

English verb conjugation is highly appreciated all over the world as it is considered quite easy. And if you think about it, you would probably agree!

Unfortunately, Italian conjugation of verbs is different—not to mention all the irregular verbs! Before panicking, or getting started with the conjugation itself, let's talk about some useful preliminary points.

First of all, in Italian, there are three groups of verbs—the verbs belonging to the *–are, -ere, and –ire* groups. That means that, at their base forms, verbs end in either –are, -ere or –ire.

Examples:

- cant<u>are</u> (to sing)

- ved<u>ere</u> (to see)

- cap<u>ire</u> (to understand)

The verb conjugation for these three groups is different, but not that much, as we will see in the next sections.

An important difference from the English language is that, if in English we must use the subject pronoun while talking or writing—e.g. <u>I</u> study Italian—in Italian the subject pronoun is not always needed, as the conjugated verb is different according to the subject pronoun it refers to.

In short, this means that in Italian you would not say "You speak English", but just "Speak English" —*parli italiano* and not *TU parli italiano* —as *parli* is the conjugated form of the verb *parlare* for the subject pronoun you (*tu*) only.

Let's explore the verb conjugation, then, *andiamo* (let's go)!

a. Essere e Avere - To be and to have

Obviously, the first two verbs we should see are two of the most used ones, to be and to have—*essere* and *avere*. And, just like in English, these two verbs are irregular in Italian as well.

Subject pronoun	essere	avere
io (I)	sono	ho
tu (you)	sei	hai
lui/lei/Lei (he/she/formal)	è	ha
noi (we)	siamo	abbiamo
voi (you)	siete	avete
loro (they)	sono	hanno

A short list of things that you should notice and learn:

- In Italian, there is no "it".

- If you want to be formal or polite, for example when speaking to someone you do not know, or who is older than you, you have to conjugate the verb according to the subject pronoun she—*Lei*.

- Please note the accent on *è* (he/she/it is).

- Please note the recurring *h* in the conjugation of the verb to have. When writing in Italian, you must not forget it, otherwise the word will take on a different meaning!

ho (I have) vs *o* (or)
hai (you have, singular) vs *ai* (to the)
ha (he/she/it has) vs *a* (to)
hanno (they have) vs *anno* (year)

b. –Are, -Ere, -Ire

When conjugating a verb, the first thing you have to do is take the verb root—i.e., the part of the verb without –are, -ere, or –ire—and then attach the endings related to the different subject pronouns.

Let's now see how to conjugate the regular verbs belonging to the –are, -ere and –ire groups in the present tense.

	Parlare (to speak)	*Cadere* (to fall)	*Sentire* (to hear)
io (I)	*parl-o*	*cad-o*	*sent-o*
tu (you)	*parl-i*	*cad-i*	*sent-i*
lui/lei/Lei (he/she/formal)	*parl-a*	*cad-e*	*sent-e*
noi (we)	*parl-iamo*	*cad-iamo*	*sent-iamo*
voi (you)	*parl-ate*	*cad-ete*	*sent-ite*
loro (they)	*parl-ano*	*cad-ono*	*sent-ono*

You might have noticed that the endings for the subject pronouns *io, tu* and *noi* are always the same, no matter the group the verb belongs to.

And now you see why in Italian subject pronouns are not commonly used when talking or writing, as they are not needed. For example, if you write *parlano,* we immediately know that the subject is they, because that is the verb ending associated to it.

Unfortunately, there are also quite a few irregular verbs. They are considered irregular as the verb root changes when conjugating the verb. Let's see the conjugation of some of the most used—and useful—irregular verbs.

	Andare (to go)	*Fare* (to do/make)	*Volere* (to want)
io (I)	vado	faccio	voglio
tu (you)	vai	fai	vuoi
lui/lei/Lei (he/she/formal)	va	fa	vuole
noi (we)	andiamo	facciamo	vogliamo
voi (you)	andate	fate	volete
loro (they)	vanno	fanno	vogliono

	Potere (can)	*Bere* (to drink)	*Finire* (to finish)
io (I)	posso	bevo	finisco
tu (you)	puoi	bevi	finisci
lui/lei/Lei (he/she/formal)	può	beve	finisce
noi (we)	possiamo	beviamo	finiamo
voi (you)	potete	bevete	finite
loro (they)	possono	bevono	finiscono

c. Frasi negative e interrogative – Negative sentences and questions

We know verb conjugation can be overwhelming, but we have some great news for you!

When it comes to creating negative sentences or questions, doing it in Italian is actually easier than in English.

For the negative sentences, in Italian, the only thing you have to do is add the adverb *non* in front of the verb, and *il gioco è fatto!* (problem solved)

Examples:

- <u>*Non*</u> *lavoro il lunedì* – I don't work on Mondays.

- <u>*Non*</u> *hanno un cane* – They don't have a dog.

It might seem hard to believe, but asking a question is even easier. You only need to add a question mark at the end of your sentence in order to transform an affirmative sentence into a question.

Examples:

- *Sei Americano* (You're American) – *Sei americano?* (Are you American?)

- *Abitano a Londra* (They live in London) – *Abitano a Londra?* (Do they live in London?)

See? *Facile come bere un bicchier d'acqua*—literally, as easy as drinking a glass of water, a common Italian expression.

IV.   I nomi – Nouns

Now that we know how to conjugate a verb in Italian, the next step is discovering how to structure a whole sentence. In order to do so, we need to learn how to use the nouns.

The first thing we should explain is that, unlike in English, Italian nouns are either **singular or plural, masculine or feminine.**

This distinction is very important, as everything—from verbs to articles and adjectives—needs to match the gender and the number of the noun it refers to.

How can you recognize masculine from feminine words, singulars from plurals?

Please note that the following are just guidelines. Most words follow these rules, but there are several exceptions.

Masculine singular words generally end with **–o**. When they become plural, they end with **–i.**

Examples:

- cavallo – cavalli (horse – horses)

- forno – forni (oven – ovens)

- tavolo – tavoli (table – tables)

On the other hand, feminine singular words generally end with **–a**. When they become plural, their ending is usually **–e.**

Examples:

- porta – porte (door – doors)

- partita – partite (match – matches)

- stanza – stanze (room – rooms)

However, we also have some singular nouns ending with **–e**, and they could be either masculine or feminine ones. When those become plural, their ending is **–i**.

Examples:

- cane – cani (masc., dog – dogs)

- canzone – canzoni (fem., song – songs)

- dente – denti (masc., tooth – teeth)

V.   Gli articoli determinativi – Definite articles

In order to properly speak and understand the Italian language, we need to learn the articles.

Once again, the English language spoiled us with only one definite article, *the*. In Italian, there are six of them.

Don't get scared, though, as their use follows specific rules and, for once, there are no exceptions!

As already anticipated, you will have to pick the right article based on the gender and the number of the word it refers to:

Articles for masculine singular words:

- **IL** = used for most of the masculine singular words beginning with a consonant. Examples: *il giubbotto* (the coat), *il pianoforte* (the piano).

- **LO** = used for masculine words beginning with s + consonant, ps, pn, gn, x, y and z. Examples: *lo zaino* (the backpack), *lo psicologo* (the psychologist), *lo yogurt* (the yogurt), *lo spazio* (the space).

Articles for masculine plural words:

- **I** = plural of IL. Examples: *i giubbotti* (the coats), *i pianoforti* (the pianos).

- **GLI** = plural of LO. Examples: *gli zaini* (the backpacks), *gli psicologi* (the psychologists), *gli yogurt* (the yogurts), *gli spazi* (the spaces).

Article for feminine singular words:

- **LA** = used for all feminine words beginning with a consonant. Examples: *la strada* (the street), *la valigia* (the suitcase), *la casa* (the house).

Article for feminine plural words:

- **LE** = plural of LA. Examples: *le strade* (the streets), *le valigie* (the suitcases), *le case* (the houses).

Article for singular words beginning with a vowel:

- **L'** = used for masculine and feminine words. Examples: *l'ape* (fem., the bee), *l'albero* (masc., the tree).

Articles for plural words beginning with a vowel:

- **GLI** = used for masculine plural words. Examples: *gli alberi* (the trees), *gli aerei* (the planes), *gli elefanti* (the elephants).

- **LE** = used for feminine plural words. Examples: *le api* (the bees), *le erbe* (the herbs), *le arti* (the arts).

VI.   Gli aggettivi – The adjectives

After having discussed articles, the only thing left, before exploring the structure of an Italian sentence, is adjectives.

In English, adjectives are invariable, which means that they never change. However, in Italian, adjectives have to match the gender and the number of the word they refer to.

In fact, an Italian adjective can have four forms—masculine singular, masculine plural, feminine singular and feminine plural—or just two—one for the singular and one for the plural.

Examples:

- *Piccolo* (masc.sing.), *piccola* (fem.sing.), *piccoli* (masc.plur.), *piccole* (fem.plur.) = small

- *Grande* (masc/fem. sing.), *grandi* (masc/fem. plur.) = big

- *Bello* (masc.sing.), *bella* (fem.sing.), *belli* (masc.plur.), *belle* (fem.plur.) = nice

- *Interessante* (masc/fem. sing.), *interessanti* (masc/fem. plur.) = interesting

Do you recognize the endings of the adjectives?

For example, if you want to say "the small house" in Italian, the first thing to do is think if the main noun—*casa*, house—is masculine or feminine, singular or plural. It is feminine and singular, so we will say *"la casa piccola"* or *"la piccola casa"*, as the adjective position is quite flexible in Italian, even though it is more common to place it after the noun it refers to.

VII.   Struttura della frase – The sentence structure

The last thing we should discuss is, obviously, how to make a sentence in Italian.

As already mentioned, Italians do not use subject pronouns that much, so, in general, a sentence will start with the verb directly.

Then, you can add whatever you want! The structure of an Italian sentence is a flexible one and can be summarized as follows:

SUBJECT + VERB + OBJECT

Examples:

- *Ho una macchina nuova* = I have a new car

- *Lucia parla inglese* = Lucia speaks English

- *Sono una ragazza italiana, ma vivo negli Stati Uniti* = I am an Italian girl, but I live in the United States

- *Nel mio tempo libero faccio sport e guardo delle serie tv* (or *"faccio sport nel mio tempo libero e guardo delle serie tv"*) = In my free time, I practice sports and I watch TV series

VIII.   Falsi amici – False friends

(Un)fortunately, there are some similar words in the Italian and the English language. Sometimes, they can really be helpful, but in some cases they are false friends, which means that their meaning is completely different in Italian than in English.

This is why we prepared a short list of the most common ones:

- *confrontare* = to compare

- *argomento* = topic

- *caldo* = warm, hot

- *delusione* = disappointment

- *attualmente* = now

- *magazzino* = warehouse

- *eventualmente* = possibly

- *educato* = polite

- *morbido* = soft

- *parenti* = relatives

- *domandare* = to ask

- *grosso* = big

- *pavimento* = floor

- *ricordo* = memory

- *romanzo* = novel

- *camera* = room

- *fabbrica* = factory

- *stampa* = press

- *avviso* = warning

Now that you know them, do not fall for these wolves in sheep's clothing!

Well, we hope that you enjoyed this short introduction to the Italian language. Even if there is much more to cover, these are the main things you should know to get started.

Now let's have some fun!

EMOZIONI (EMOTIONS)

1) **felice** (happy)
   feh-LEE-che

2) **triste** (sad)
   TREE-steh

3) **emozionato** (excited)
   eh-moh-dzeoh-NAH-toh

4) **arrabbiato** (angry)
   ahr-rahb-BEEAH-toh

5) **sorpreso** (surprised)
   sohr-PREH-soh

6) **preoccupato** (concerned)
   preh-ohc-coo-PAH-toh

7) **impaurito** (scared)
   im-pah-oo-REE-toh

8) **curioso** (curious)
   coo-REEOH-soh

9) **divertito** (amused)
   dee-vehr-TEE-toh

10) **confuso** (confused)
    cohn-FOO-soh

11) **malato** (sick)
    mah-LAH-toh

12) **impertinente** (naughty)
    ee-mpehr-tee-NEHN-teh

13) **serio** (serious)
    SEH-ree-oh

14) **concentrato** (focused)
    kohn-chen-TRAH-toh

15) **annoiato** (bored)
    ahn-noh-EEAH-toh

16) **sopraffatto** (overwhelmed)
    soh-prahf-FAHT-toh

17) **innamorato** (in love)
    een-nah-moh-RAH-toh

18) **imbarazzato** (ashamed)
    eem-bah-rah-DZAH-toh

19) **ansioso** (anxious)
    ahn-SEEOH-soh

20) **disgustato** (disgusted)
    dee-sgoo-STAH-toh

21) **offeso** (offended)
    ohf-FEH-soh

22) **ferito** (sore)
    feh-REE-toh

Mi sembri molto innamorato della tua ragazza
You seem really in love with your girlfriend.

Oggi sono malato; ho febbre e mal di testa.
Today I'm sick; I have a fever and a headache.

Erano così sorpresi di vederci!
They were so surprised to see us!

LA FAMIGLIA (THE FAMILY)

1) **nonni** (grandparents)
NOHN-nee

2) **nonna** (grandmother)
NOHN-nah

3) **nonno** (grandfather)
NOHN-noh

4) **zio** (uncle)
DZEE-oh

5) **madre** (mother)
MAH-dreh

6) **padre** (father)
PAH-dreh

7) **zia** (aunt)
DZEE-ah

8) **cugino** (cousin)
coo-GEE-noh

9) **fratello** (brother)
frah-TEHL-loh

10) **io** (me)
eeoh

11) **marito/moglie** (husband/wife)
mah-REE-toh/MOH-lleh

12) **sorella** (sister)
soh-REHL-lah

13) **cugina** (cousin)
coo-GEE-nah

14) **nipote** (nephew)
nee-POH-teh

15) **figlio** (son)
FEE-lloh

16) **figlia** (daughter)
FEE-llah

17) **nipote** (niece)
nee-POH-teh

18) **nipote** (grandson)
nee-POH-teh

19) **nipote** (granddaughter)
nee-POH-teh

20) **secondo cugino** (second cousin)
she-KOHN-doh coo-GEE-noh

- **Parenti acquisiti (In-laws)**
  – **Parenti (Relatives)**

  pah-REHN-tee ah-cooee-SEE-tee

  – pah-REHN-tee

21) **suocero** (father-in-law)
soo-OH-ceh-roh

22) **suocera** (mother-in-law)
soo-OH-ceh-rah

23) **cognato** (brother-in-law)
koh-ÑAH-toh

24) **cognata** (sister-in-law)
koh-ÑAH-tah

25) **nuora** (daughter-in-law)
noo-OH-rah

26) **genero** (son-in-law)
GEH-neh-roh

27) **zio acquisito** (uncle-in-law)
DZEE-oh ah-coo-ee-SEE-toh

28) **zia acquisita** (aunt-in-law)
DZEE-ah ah-coo-ee-SEE-tah

Ho una sorella e due fratelli che hanno due figli ciascuno.
I have a sister and two brothers, who have two sons each.

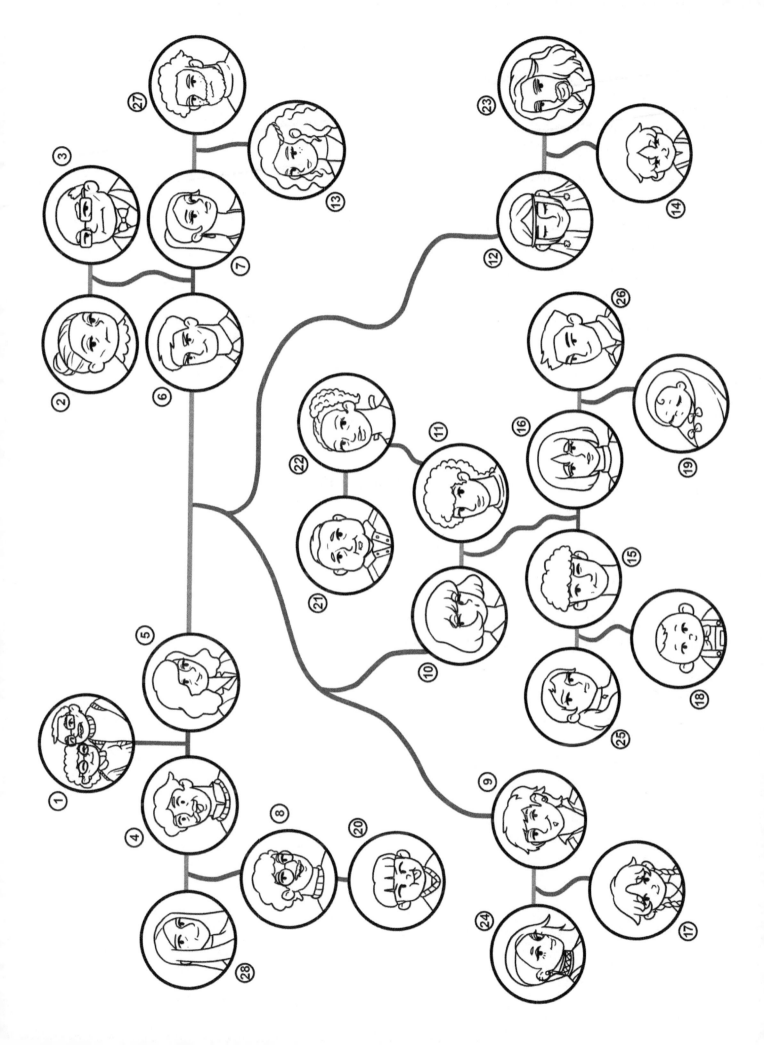

RELAZIONI (RELATIONSHIPS)

1) **coppia sposata** (married couple)
   KOHP-peeah spoh-SAH-tah

2) **uomo sposato** (married man)
   oo-OH-moh spoh-SAH-toh

3) **donna sposata** (married woman)
   DOHN-nah spoh-SAH-tah

4) **coppia divorziata** (divorced couple)
   KOHP-peeah dee-vohr-DZEAH-tah

5) **ex moglie** (ex-wife)
   ehx MOH-lleh

6) **ex marito** (ex-husband)
   ehx mah-REE-toh

7) **amico** (friend)
   ah-MEE-koh

8) **ragazza** (girlfriend)
   rah-GAH-dzah

9) **ragazzo** (boyfriend)
   rah-GAH-dzoh

10) **vicino** (neighbor)
    vee-CHI-noh

11) **single** (single)
    as in English

12) **divorziato/a** (divorcé/divorcée)
    dee-vohr-DZEAH-toh

13) **vedovo** (widower)
    VEH-doh-voh

14) **vedova** (widow)
    VEH-doh-vah

La mia amica Giulia ha un ex marito che si chiama Marco.
My friend Giulia has an ex-husband called Marco.

Il suo ragazzo è un medico.
His/her boyfriend is a doctor.

Sono single; non ho un ragazzo, ma molti amici!
I am single; I do not have a boyfriend, but I have many friends!

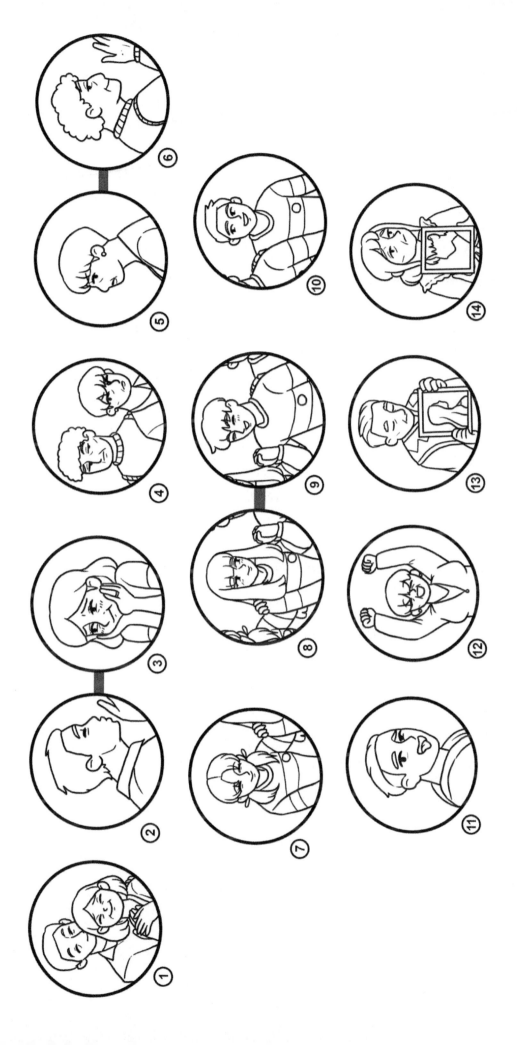

VALORI (VALUES)

1) **rispetto** (respect)
   ree-SPEHT-toh

2) **gratitudine** (gratitude)
   grah-tee-TOO-dee-neh

3) **tolleranza** (tolerance)
   tohl-leh-RAHN-dzah

4) **collaborazione** (collaboration)
   kohl-lah-boh-rah-DZEOH-neh

5) **onestà** (honesty)
   oh-neh-STAH

6) **moderazione** (temperance)
   moh-deh-rah-DZEOH-neh

7) **responsabilità** (responsibility)
   reh-spohn-sah-bee-lee-TAH

8) **fede** (faith)
   FEH-deh

9) **coraggio** (courage)
   coh-RAH-jeoh

10) **gentilezza** (kindness)
    gehn-tee-LEH-dzah

11) **impegno** (commitment)
    eem-PEH-ñoh

12) **entusiasmo** (enthusiasm)
    ehn-too-SEEAH-smoh

13) **fiducia** (trust)
    fee-DUH-chi-ah

14) **puntualità** (punctuality)
    poon-too-ah-lee-TAH

La puntualità non è il punto forte di mio fratello.
Punctuality is not my brother's speciality.

Credo fermamente nell'onestà e nella gentilezza.
I strongly believe in honesty and kindness.

Dovremmo praticare la gratitutine ogni giorno.
We should express gratitude every day.

IL CORPO UMANO (THE HUMAN BODY)

1) **testa** (head)
TEH-stah

2) **capelli** (hair)
kah-PEHL-lee

3) **faccia/viso** (face)
FAH-chi-ah/VEE-soh

4) **fronte** (forehead)
FROHN-teh

5) **orecchio** (ear)
oh-REH-key-oh

6) **occhio** (eye)
OH-key-oh

7) **naso** (nose)
NAH-soh

8) **guancia** (cheek)
goo-AHN-chi-ah

9) **bocca** (mouth)
BOH-kah

10) **mento** (chin)
MEHN-toh

11) **collo** (neck)
KOHL-loh

12) **schiena** (back)
skee-EH-nah

13) **petto** (chest)
PEHT-toh

14) **spalla** (shoulder)
SPAHL-lah

15) **braccio** (arm)
BRAH-chi-oh

16) **avambraccio** (forearm)
ah-vahm-BRAH-chi-oh

17) **mano** (hand)
MAH-noh

18) **addome** (abdomen)
ahd-DOH-meh

19) **vita** (waist)
VEE-tah

20) **fianco** (hip)
fee-AHN-koh

21) **gamba** (leg)
GAHM-bah

22) **coscia** (thigh)
KOH-she-ah

23) **ginocchio** (knee)
gee-NOH-key-oh

24) **polpaccio** (calf)
pohl-PAH-chi-oh

25) **stinco** (shin)
STEEN-koh

26) **piede** (foot)
pee-EH-deh

Ho i capelli biondi e gli occhi blu.
I have blond hair and blue eyes.

Ti sei fatto male al piede?
Did you hurt your foot?

Abbiamo tutti le gambe lunghe in famiglia!
We all have long legs in the family!

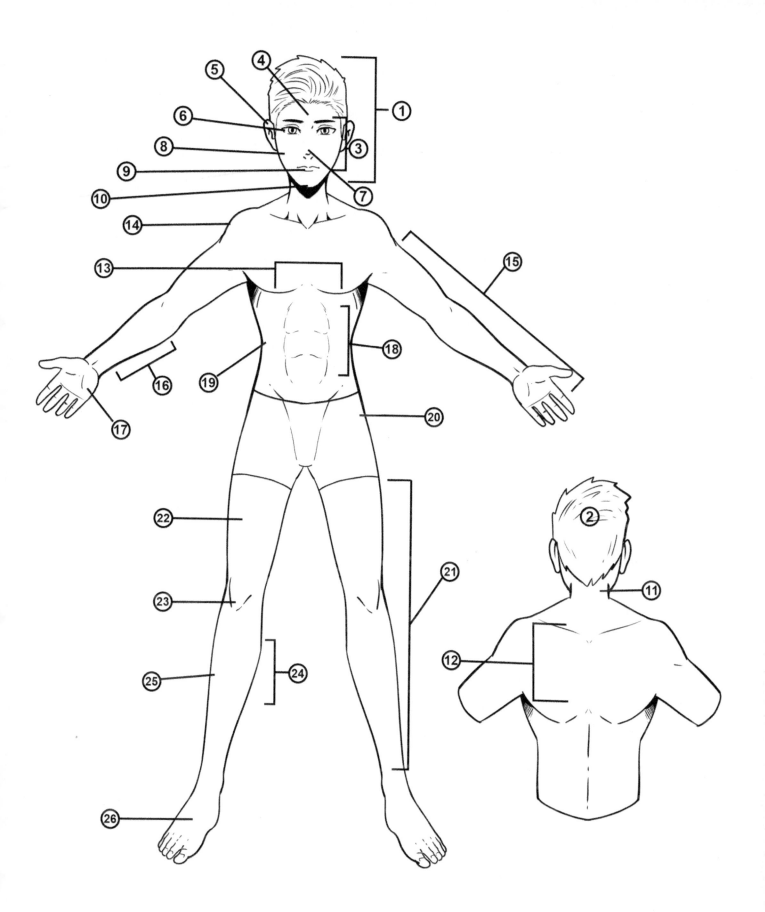

NEL CORPO UMANO (INSIDE THE HUMAN BODY)

1) **pelle** (skin)
PEHL-leh

2) **muscoli** (muscles)
MOO-skoh-lee

3) **ossa** (bones)
OHS-sah

4) **cervello** (brain)
che-RVEHL-loh

5) **tiroide** (thyroid)
tee-ROH-ee-deh

6) **vene** (veins)
VEH-neh

7) **arterie** (arteries)
ahr-TEH-ree-eh

8) **cuore** (heart)
coo-OH-reh

9) **polmoni** (lungs)
pohl-MOH-nee

10) **stomaco** (stomach)
STOH-mah-koh

11) **esofago** (esophagus)
eh-SOH-fah-goh

12) **pancreas** (pancreas)
PAHN-kreh-ahs

13) **fegato** (liver)
FEH-gah-toh

14) **intestino tenue** (small intestine)
een-teh-STEE-noh TEH-noo-eh

15) **intestino crasso** (large intestine)
een-teh-STEE-noh KRAHS-soh

16) **cistifellea** (gallbladder)
chi-stee-FEHL-leh-ah

17) **reni** (kidneys)
REH-nee

18) **vescica** (urinary bladder)
veh-SHE-kah

Smetti di fumare per la salute dei tuoi polmoni!
Stop smoking for the sake of your lungs!

Mia madre ha un cuore grande.
My mother has a big heart.

Ho la pelle chiara ma mi abbronzo d'estate.
I have pale skin, but I tan in summer.

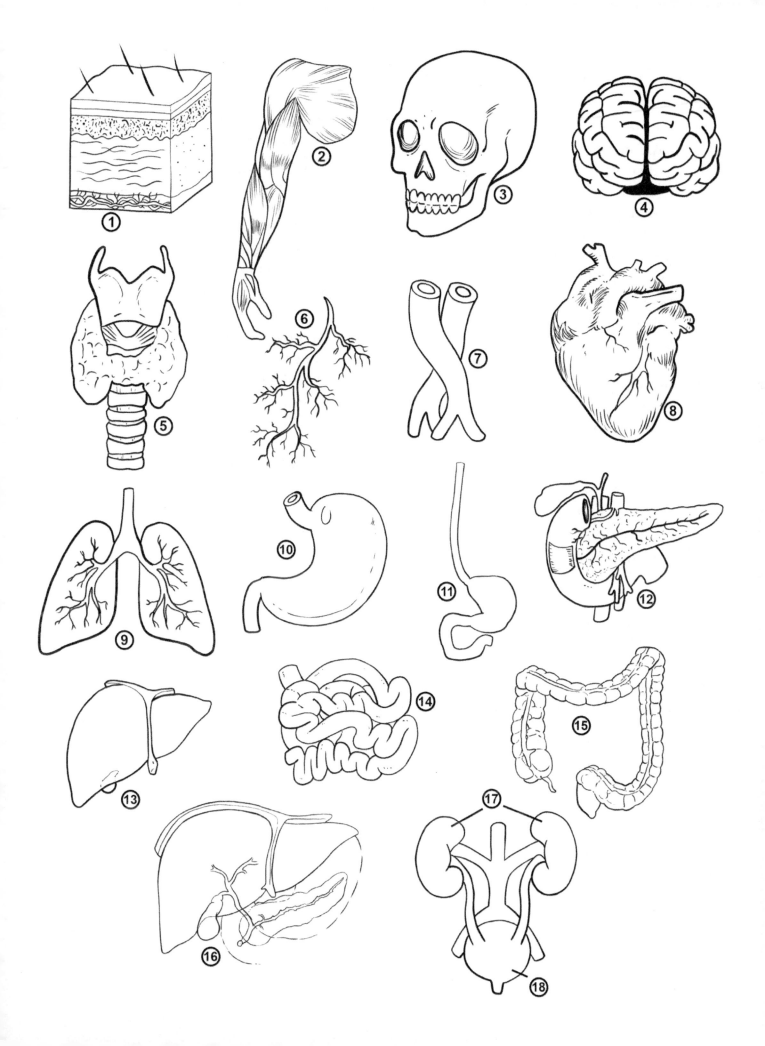

ANIMALI DOMESTICI (PETS)

1) **cane** (dog)
KAH-neh

2) **gatto** (cat)
GAHT-toh

3) **furetto** (ferret)
foo-REHT-toh

4) **maialino nano** (mini pig/teacup pig)
mah-eeah-LEE-noh NAH-noh

5) **cavallo** (horse)
kah-VAHL-loh

6) **pesce angelo** (angelfish)
PEH-scheh AHN-geh-loh

7) **pesce pagliaccio** (clown fish)
PEH-scheh pah-llee-AH-chi-oh

8) **pesce rosso** (goldfish)
PEH-scheh ROHS-soh

9) **criceto** (hamster)
kree-CHE-toh

10) **porcellino d'India** (guinea pig)
pohr-chel-LEE-noh DEEN-dee-ah

11) **topo** (mouse)
TOH-poh

12) **coniglio** (rabbit)
koh-NEE-lleeoh

13) **riccio** (hedgehog)
REE-chi-oh

14) **tarantola** (tarantula)
tah-RAHN-toh-lah

15) **colonia di formiche** (ant colony)
koh-LOH-neeah dee fohr-MEE-keh

16) **tartaruga** (tortoise)
tahr-tah-ROO-gah

17) **serpente** (snake)
sehr-PEHN-teh

18) **camaleonte** (chameleon)
kah-mah-leh-OHN-teh

19) **iguana** (iguana)
ee-goo-AH-nah

20) **canarino** (canary)
cah-nah-REE-noh

21) **pappagallo** (parrot)
pahp-pah-GAHL-loh

22) **cocorita** (parakeet)
koh-koh-REE-tah

Ho paura dei serpenti.
I am scared of snakes.

Il suo sogno è avere un maialino nano nel giardino!
His/her dream is having a mini pig in the garden!

Il nostro pappagallo non sa parlare. Che fregatura!
Our parrot cannot speak. What a bummer!

LO ZOO (THE ZOO)

1) **elefante** (elephant)
   eh-leh-PHAN-teh

2) **rinoceronte** (rhinoceros)
   ree-noh-che-ROHN-teh

3) **giraffa** (giraffe)
   gee-RAH-phah

4) **zebra** (zebra)
   DZEH-brah

5) **ippopotamo** (hippopotamus)
   eep-poh-POH-tah-moh

6) **ghepardo** (cheetah)
   gheh-PAHR-doh

7) **tigre** (tiger)
   TEE-greh

8) **leone** (lion)
   leh-OH-neh

9) **scimpanzé** (chimpanzee)
   shem-pahn-DZEH

10) **orangotango** (orangutan)
    oh-rahn-goh-THAN-goh

11) **babbuino** (baboon)
    bah-boo-EE-noh

12) **canguro** (kangaroo)
    kahn-GOO-roh

13) **koala** (koala)
    koh-AH-lah

14) **lemure** (lemur)
    LEH-moo-reh

Il mio animale preferito è la tigre.
My favorite animal is the tiger.

Il babbuino mi ha rubato la banana!
The baboon stole my banana!

Dobbiamo preservare gli elefanti.
We must preserve elephants.

UCCELLI (BIRDS)

1) **struzzo** (ostrich)
   STROO-dzoh

2) **pavone** (peacock)
   pah-VOH-neh

3) **tacchino** (turkey)
   tah-KEE-noh

4) **gallo** (rooster)
   GAHL-loh

5) **papera** (duck)
   PAH-peh-rah

6) **cigno** (swan)
   CHI-ñoh

7) **pellicano** (pelican)
   peh-lee-KAH-noh

8) **fenicottero** (flamingo)
   feh-nee-KOH-teh-roh

9) **piccione** (pigeon)
   pee-chi-OH-neh

10) **gufo** (owl)
    GOO-phoh

11) **avvoltoio** (vulture)
    ah-vohl-TOH-eeoh

12) **aquila** (eagle)
    AH-cooee-lah

13) **gabbiano** (seagull)
    gah-bee-AH-noh

14) **corvo** (crow)
    KOHR-voh

15) **tucano** (toucan)
    too-KAH-noh

16) **pinguino** (penguin)
    peen-goo-EE-noh

17) **picchio** (woodpecker)
    PEE-keeoh

18) **ara** (macaw)
    AH-rah

19) **colibrì** (hummingbird)
    koh-lee-BREE

20) **kiwi** (kiwi)
    KEE-oo-ee

Hai visto quel gufo sull'albero?
Did you see that owl on the tree?

Ci sono più piccioni che persone in piazza.
There are more pigeons than people in the square.

Guarda! Il pavone sta facendo la ruota!
Look! The peacock is doing a cartwheel!

QUIZ #1

Use arrows to match the corresponding translations:

a. horse	1. nonno
b. concerned	2. tigre
c. arm	3. gamba
d. cat	4. cervello
e. brain	5. cavallo
f. mother	6. felice
g. penguin	7. muscoli
h. grandfather	8. braccio
i. happy	9. marito
j. trust	10. fede
k. tiger	11. preoccupato
l. muscles	12. cane
m. husband	13. pinguino
n. dog	14. fiducia
o. leg	15. gatto
p. faith	16. madre

Fill in the blank spaces with the options below (use each word only once):

Francesco stava giocando a calcio con il suo _____, quando suo _____ lo ha chiamato per dirgli di tornare a casa. Suo fratello, Carlo, sembrava molto _____ al telefono. Dopo poco lo chiamano anche i _____. Francesco, che è un ragazzo _____, prende subito il pallone e torna a casa, dove trova sua _____ Lidia con la _____ sul _____. Era caduta dalle scale! Insieme a Carlo, aiutano Lidia a salire in macchina. Arrivano all'ospedale e, per fortuna, non era niente di grave. Lidia, infatti, non aveva battuto la _____ durante la caduta. I medici le hanno detto che deve solo riposare! Adesso è sul divano a guardare un documentario sugli _____ con il suo _____ persiano e sua _____.

testa

nonni

ansioso

animali

madre

preoccupato

gatto

piede

cane

sorella

fratello

mano

RETTILI E ANFIBI (REPTILES AND AMPHIBIANS)

- **Rettili (Reptiles)**
  REH-tee-lee

1) **anaconda** (anaconda)
   ah-nah-KOHN-dah

2) **cobra reale** (king cobra)
   KOH-brah reh-AH-leh

3) **serpente a sonagli** (rattlesnake)
   sehr-PEHN-teh ah soh-NAH-llee

4) **serpente corallo** (coral snake)
   sehr-PEHN-teh koh-RAHL-loh

5) **lucertola cornuta** (horned lizard)
   loo-CHER-toh-lah kohr-NOO-tah

6) **clamidosauro** (frill-necked lizard)
   klah-mee-doh-SAH-oo-roh

7) **basilisco comune** (common
   basilisk/Jesus Christ lizard)
   bah-see-LEE-skoh koh-MOO-neh

8) **drago di Komodo** (Komodo dragon)
   DRAH-goh dee koh-MOH-doh

9) **coccodrillo** (crocodile)
   koh-koh-DREEL-loh

10) **gaviale** (gharial/gavial)
    gah-vee-AH-leh

11) **tartaruga marina** (sea turtle)
    tahr-tah-ROO-gah mah-REE-nah

- **Anfibi (Amphibians)**
  Ahn-PHE-bee

12) **salamandra** (salamander)
    sah-lah-MAHN-drah

13) **rana golia** (Goliath frog)
    RAH-nah goh-LEE-ah

Hai mai visto un clamidosauro?
Have you ever seen a frill-necked lizard?

Il serpente a sonagli si riconosce dalla sua coda.
You can recognize a rattlesnake by its tail.

I coccodrilli sono il mio peggior incubo!
Crocodiles are my worst nightmare!

INSETTI E ARACNIDI (INSECTS AND ARACHNIDS)

- **Insetti (Insects)**
  een-SEH-tee

1) **ape** (bee)
   AH-peh

2) **calabrone** (bumblebee)
   kah-lah-BROH-neh

3) **vespa** (wasp)
   VEH-spah

4) **scarabeo** (beetle)
   skah-rah-BEH-oh

5) **farfalla** (butterfly)
   phar-PHAHL-lah

6) **falena** (moth)
   pha-LEH-nah

7) **libellula** (dragonfly)
   lee-BEHL-oo-lah

8) **coccinella** (ladybug)
   koh-chi-NEHL-ah

9) **lucciola** (firefly)
   LOO-chi-oh-lah

10) **scarafaggio** (cockroach)
    skah-rah-FAH-jeeoh

11) **tafano** (horsefly)
    tah-PHA-noh

12) **mosca** (fly)
    MOH-skah

13) **zanzara** (mosquito)
    dzahn-DZAH-rah

14) **cavalletta** (grasshopper)
    kah-vah-LEHT-tah

15) **grillo** (cricket)
    GREEL-loh

- **Aracnidi (Arachnids)**
  ah-RAHK-nee-dee

16) **scorpione** (scorpion)
    skohr-pee-OH-neh

17) **ragno** (spider)
    RAH-ñoh

18) **vedova nera** (Southern black widow)
    VEH-doh-vah NEH-rah

Le coccinelle portano fortuna!
Ladybugs bring good luck!

Aiuto! Sono allergico alle api!
Help! I am allergic to bees!

Non c'è niente che le faccia più paura dei ragni.
There is nothing she is more afraid of than spiders.

MAMMIFERI I (MAMMALS I)

1) **pipistrello** (bat)
   pee-pee-STREH-loh

2) **ornitorinco** (platypus)
   ohr-nee-toh-REEN-koh

3) **orca** (killer whale/orca)
   OHR-kah

4) **delfino** (dolphin)
   dehl-PHE-noh

5) **castoro** (beaver)
   kah-STOH-roh

6) **marmotta** (groundhog)
   mahr-MOH-tah

7) **talpa** (mole)
   TAHL-pah

8) **scoiattolo** (squirrel)
   skoh-EEAHT-toh-loh

9) **donnola** (weasel)
   DOHN-noh-lah

10) **opossum** (possum/opossum)
   oh-POH-soom

11) **ratto** (rat)
   RAHT-toh

12) **lepre** (hare)
   LEH-preh

13) **tasso** (badger)
   TAHS-soh

14) **puzzola** (skunk)
   POO-dzoh-lah

15) **leopardo** (leopard)
   leh-oh-PAHR-doh

Una talpa mi ha distrutto l'orto la scorsa notte.
A mole destroyed my vegetable garden last night.

Gli scoiattoli sono adorabili, ma possono mordere!
Squirrels are adorable, but they can bite!

Hai mai visto un delfino nel mare?
Have you ever seen a dolphin in the sea?

MAMMIFERI II (MAMMALS II)

1) **orso** (bear)
   OHR-soh

2) **iena** (hyena)
   ee-EH-nah

3) **sciacallo** (jackal)
   she-ah-KAHL-loh

4) **mucca** (cow)
   MOO-kah

5) **toro** (bull)
   TOH-roh

6) **volpe** (fox)
   VOHL-peh

7) **bufalo** (buffalo)
   BOO-fah-loh

8) **alce** (elk/moose)
   AHL-che

9) **pecora** (sheep)
   PEH-koh-rah

10) **capra** (goat)
    KAH-prah

11) **gazzella** (gazelle)
    gah-DZEHL-lah

12) **lupo** (wolf)
    LOO-poh

13) **scimmia** (monkey)
    SHE-meeah

14) **ariete** (ram)
    ah-ree-EH-teh

15) **asino** (donkey)
    AH-see-noh

Mio fratello è furbo come una volpe!
My brother is as sly as a fox!

Le pecore producono una lana morbidissima.
Sheep produce a very soft wool.

Ci sono degli orsi in Italia?
Are there any bears in Italy?

PESCI E MOLLUSCHI (FISH AND MOLLUSKS)

- **Pesci (Fish)**
  PEH-she

1) **squalo balena** (whale shark)
   scoo-AH-loh bah-LEH-nah

2) **squalo bianco** (white shark)
   scoo-AH-loh bee-AHN-koh

3) **squalo martello** (hammerhead shark)
   scoo-AH-loh mahr-TEH-loh

4) **pesce spada** (swordfish/marlin)
   PEH-sche SPAH-dah

5) **barracuda** (barracuda)
   bahr-rah-COO-dah

6) **pesce palla** (pufferfish)
   PEH-sche PAHL-lah

7) **pesce gatto** (catfish)
   PEH-sche GAHT-toh

8) **piranha** (piranha)
   pee-RAH-ñah

9) **pesce volante** (flying fish)
   PEH-sche voh-LAHN-teh

10) **murena** (moray eel)
    moo-REH-nah

11) **manta** (manta ray)
    MAHN-tah

12) **cavalluccio marino** (seahorse)
    kah-vah-LOO-chi-oh mah-REE-noh

- **Molluschi (Mollusks)**
  moh-LOO-skee

13) **calamaro** (squid)
    kah-lah-MAH-roh

14) **seppia** (cuttlefish)
    SEH-pee-ah

15) **polpo** (octopus)
    POHL-poh

16) **ostrica** (oyster)
    OH-stree-kah

17) **vongola** (clam)
    VOHN-goh-lah

18) **nautilo** (nautilus)
    NAH-oo-tee-loh

19) **lumaca** (snail)
    loo-MAH-kah

20) **lumaca di mare** (slug)
    loo-MAH-kah dee MAH-reh

Adoro le vongole, ma non posso mangiarle perché sono intollerante.
I love clams, but I cannot eat them as I am intolerant.

Gli squali sono maestosi e terrificanti al tempo stesso.
Sharks are majestic and terrifying at the same time.

Oggi hanno fatto un'immersione e hanno visto molte murene.
Today they went diving and they saw many moray eels.

VESTITI I (CLOTHING I)

1) **impermeabile** (raincoat)
eem-pehr-meh-AH-bee-leh

2) **felpa** (hoodie)
FEHL-pah

3) **giacca** (jacket)
jee-AH-kah

4) **jeans** (jeans)
as in English

5) **boxer** (boxer shorts)
BOH-xehr

6) **stivali** (boots)
stee-VAH-lee

7) **orecchini** (earrings)
oh-reh-KEY-nee

8) **maglione** (sweater)
mah-LLOH-neh

9) **collana** (necklace)
kohl-LAH-nah

10) **reggiseno** (bra)
reh-jee-SEH-noh

11) **leggings** (leggings)
as in English

12) **calzini** (socks)
kahl-DZEE-nee

13) **maglietta** (T-shirt/top)
mah-LLEH-tah

14) **braccialetto** (bracelet)
brah-chi-ah-LEHT-toh

15) **pantaloncini** (shorts)
pahn-tah-lohn-CHI-nee

16) **mutande** (panties)
moot-AHN-deh

17) **cappotto** (coat)
kahp-POHT-toh

18) **vestito** (dress)
veh-STEE-toh

19) **borsa** (purse)
BOHR-sah

20) **sandali** (sandals)
SAHN-dah-lee

Non porto né collane né braccialetti.
I do not wear necklaces or bracelets.

Fuori fa freddo! Metti un cappotto invernale.
It is cold outside! Put a winter coat on.

Penso che pioverà presto. Non dimenticare l'impermeabile.
I think it will rain soon. Do not forget the raincoat.

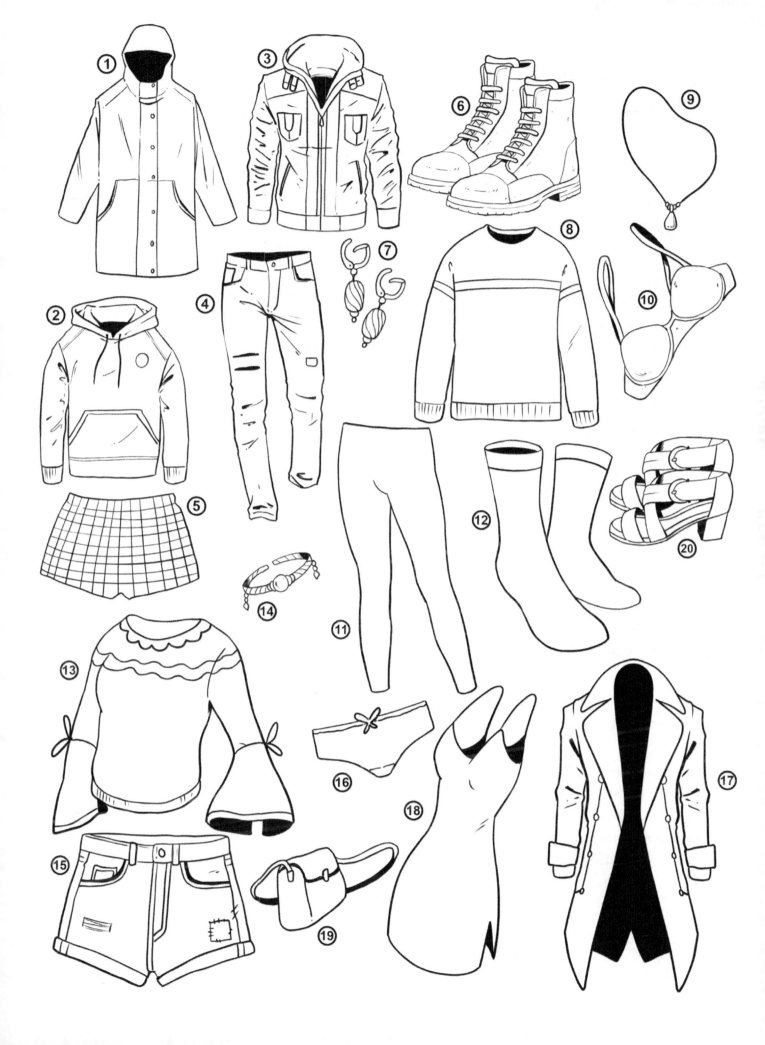

VESTITI II (CLOTHING II)

1) **cappello** (hat)
kah-PEHL-loh

2) **smoking** (tuxedo/smoking jacket)
SMOH-king

3) **papillon** (bow tie)
pah-pee-YOHN

4) **scarpe** (shoes)
SKAHR-peh

5) **completo** (suit)
kohm-PLEH-toh

6) **camicia** (shirt/blouse)
kah-MEE-chi-ah

7) **cravatta** (tie)
krah-VAH-tah

8) **valigetta** (briefcase/case)
vah-lee-JEHT-tah

9) **camicia a maniche lunghe** (long-sleeved shirt/blouse)
kah-MEE-chi-ah ah MAH-nee-keh LOON-gheh

10) **reggiseno sportivo** (sports bra)
reh-jee-SEH-noh spohr-TEE-voh

11) **pantaloni** (trousers/pants)
pahn-tah-LOH-nee

12) **cintura** (belt)
chin-TOO-rah

13) **anello** (ring)
ah-NEHL-loh

14) **maglietta a maniche corte** (T-shirt)
mah-LLEHT-tah ah MAH-nee-keh KOHR-teh

15) **gonna** (skirt)
GOHN-nah

16) **sciarpa** (scarf)
she-AHR-pah

17) **orologio** (watch)
oh-roh-LOH-jeeoh

18) **pantaloni da lavoro** (cargo pants)
pahn-tah-LOH-nee dah lah-VOH-roh

19) **portafoglio** (wallet)
pohr-tah-FOH-llee-oh

20) **ombrello** (umbrella)
ohm-BREHL-loh

Non esco mai da casa senza il mio orologio.
I never leave home without my watch.

Una mia amica ha perso il portafoglio al centro commerciale.
A friend of mine lost her wallet at the mall.

Per il matrimonio devi comprare un completo elegante.
For the wedding, you must buy a smart suit.

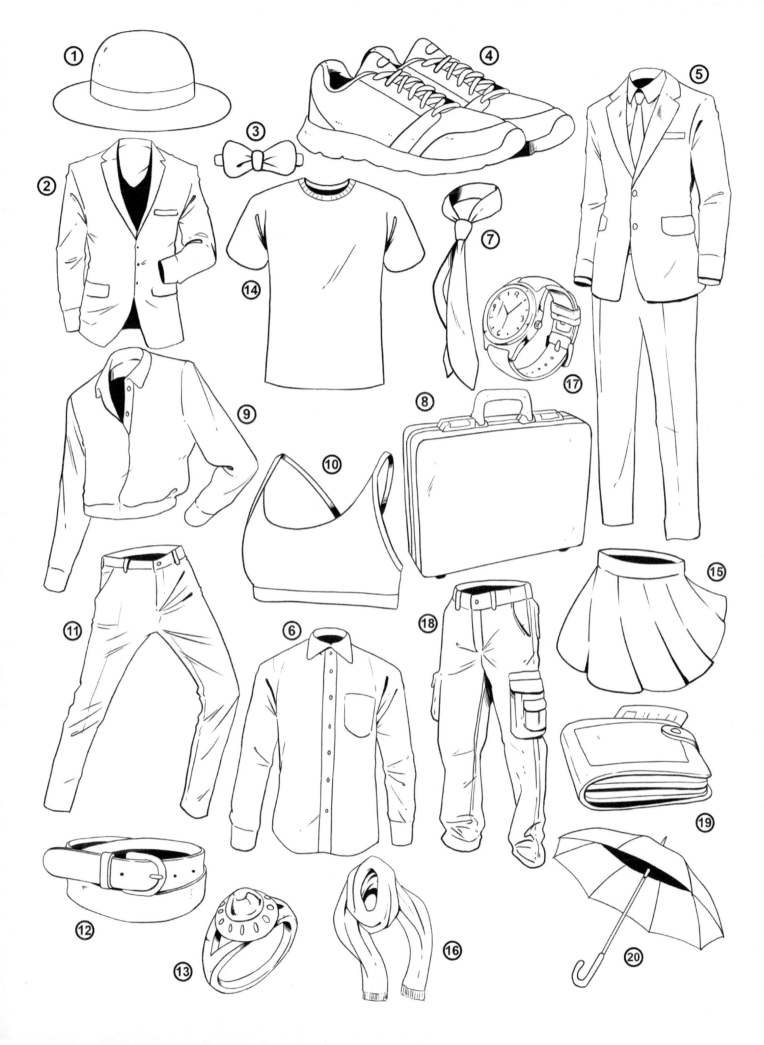

IL TEMPO (THE WEATHER)

1) **soleggiato** (sunny)
   soh-leh-JEEAH-toh

2) **caldo** (hot)
   KAHL-doh

3) **tempesta di sabbia** (sandstorm)
   tehm-PEH-stah dee SAHB-bee-ah

4) **nuvoloso** (cloudy)
   noo-voh-LOH-soh

5) **mite** (mild)
   MEE-teh

6) **nebbioso** (foggy/misty)
   neh-bee-OH-soh

7) **piovoso** (rainy)
   pee-oh-VOH-soh

8) **fresco** (cool)
   FREH-skoh

9) **goccia di pioggia** (raindrop)
   GOH-che-ah dee pee-OH-jeeah

10) **umido** (humid)
    OO-mee-doh

11) **tempesta** (storm)
    tehm-PEH-stah

12) **fulmine** (lightning)
    FOOL-mee-neh

13) **ventoso** (windy)
    vehn-TOH-soh

14) **nevoso** (snowy)
    neh-VOH-soh

15) **freddo** (cold)
    FREH-doh

16) **fiocco di neve** (snowflake)
    fee-OH-koh dee NEH-veh

Il fine settimana piove sempre. Che sfortuna.
It always rains on the weekend. How unlucky.

Oggi fa caldo ed è soleggiato. La giornata perfetta!
Today it is hot and sunny. The perfect day!

Il mio cane ha paura delle tempeste con i fulmini.
My dog is afraid of storms with lightning.

LE STAGIONI - PRIMAVERA (THE SEASONS – SPRING)

1) **giardino** (garden)
   jee-ahr-DEE-noh

2) **bocciolo** (blossom)
   boh-chi-OH-loh

3) **picnic** (picnic)
   PEEK-neek

4) **parco** (park)
   PAHR-koh

5) **giro in bici** (bike ride)
   GEE-roh een BEE-chi

6) **limonata** (lemonade)
   lee-moh-NAH-tah

7) **mercatino dell'usato** (flea market)
   mehr-kah-TEE-noh dehl-oo-SAH-toh

8) **viaggio in auto** (roadtrip)
   vee-AH-jeoh een AH-oo-toh

9) **dipingere sassi** (to paint rocks)
   dee-PEEN-jeh-reh SAHS-see

10) **piantare dei fiori** (to plant some flowers)
    pee-ahn-TAH-reh DEH-ee fee-OH-ree

11) **far volare un aquilone** (to fly a kite)
    phahr voh-LAH-reh oon ah-coo-ee-LOH-neh

12) **partecipare a un barbecue** (to attend a barbecue)
    pahr-teh-chi-PAH-reh ah oon BAHR-beh-key-oo

La cosa che preferisco dell'estate? Partecipare ai barbecue con i miei amici!
The thing I prefer about summer? Attending barbecues with my friends!

Tua sorella ha sete. Comprale una limonata fresca per favore.
Your sister is thirsty. Buy her a fresh lemonade, please.

Andiamo a fare un giro in bici nel pomeriggio?
Shall we go on a bike ride in the afternoon?

LE STAGIONI - ESTATE (THE SEASONS – SUMMER)

1) **andare in campeggio** (to go camping)
   ahn-DAH-reh een kahm-PEH-jeoh

2) **parco acquatico** (water park)
   PAHR-koh ah-coo-AH-tee-koh

3) **attività all'aperto** (outdoor activities)
   aht-tee-vee-TAH ahl ah-PEHR-toh

4) **piscina** (swimming pool)
   pee-SHE-nah

5) **nuotare** (to swim)
   noo-oh-TAH-reh

6) **abbronzarsi** (to get tanned)
   ah-brohn-DZAHR-see

7) **protezione solare** (sunscreen)
   proh-the-DZEEOH-neh soh-LAH-reh

8) **repellente per insetti** (insect repellent)
   reh-pehl-LEHN-teh pehr een-SEHT-tee

9) **lago** (lake)
   LAH-goh

10) **bagnino** (lifesaver/lifeguard)
    bah-ÑEE-noh

11) **castello di sabbia** (sandcastle)
    kah-STEHL-loh dee SAHB-bee-ah

12) **fare trekking** (to go on a hike)
    PHA-reh TREH-king

Mentre ci abbronziamo, perché non fate un castello di sabbia?
While we get tanned, why don't you make a sandcastle?

Non so nuotare.
I cannot swim.

Da bambino andavo sempre in campeggio con i miei genitori.
As a child, I always went camping with my parents.

QUIZ #2

Use arrows to match the corresponding translations:

a. suit	1. gonna
b. to attend a barbecue	2. tempesta
c. skirt	3. ratto
d. dolphin	4. completo
e. butterfly	5. pantaloni
f. pants	6. squalo
g. storm	7. farfalla
h. socks	8. primavera
i. rat	9. delfino
j. swimming pool	10. partecipare a un barbecue
k. spider	11. mosca
l. shark	12. soleggiato
m. shoes	13. calzini
n. fly	14. scarpe
o. spring	15. ragno
p. sunny	16. piscina

Fill in the blank spaces with the options below (use each word only once):

La mia stagione preferita è l'_____. Fa _____, il _____ dell'inverno è solo un brutto ricordo, e posso andare in _____ con i miei amici per _____ la mattina o il pomeriggio. Un'altra cosa che mi piace fare in compagnia sono i _____al _____. Ognuno porta qualcosa di diverso da mangiare. Adoro andare al mare e vedere gli animali marini. Una volta ho persino visto dei _____ che saltavano tra le onde! Gli animali che non vorrei vedere, però, sono lo _____ e la _____. Ho troppa paura! La mia cosa preferita da bere è la _____ o un bicchiere di acqua ghiacciata, e da mangiare amo i frutti di mare come le _____.

vongole

limonata

parco

estate

delfini

murena

caldo

picnic

squalo

piscina

freddo

nuotare

LE STAGIONI – AUTUNNO (THE SEASONS – FALL/AUTUMN)

1) **cambiamento delle foglie** (changing leaves)
kahm-bee-ah-MEHN-toh DEHL-leh FOH-lleh

2) **raccogliere foglie** (to collect leaves)
rah-KOH-lleh-reh FOH-lleh

3) **zucca** (pumpkin)
DZOO-kah

4) **intagliare zucche** (to carve pumpkins)
een-tah-LLAH-reh DZOO-keh

5) **raccogliere mele** (apple picking)
rah-KOH-lleh-reh MEH-leh

6) **costume di Halloween** (Halloween costume)
koh-STOO-meh dee ahl-loh-OOEEN

7) **dolcetti di Halloween** (Halloween candy)
dohl-CHE-tee dee ahl-loh-OOEEN

8) **candele profumate** (scented candles)
kahn-DEH-leh proh-foo-MAH-teh

9) **cena del Ringraziamento** (Thanksgiving dinner)
CHE-nah dehl reen-grah-dzee-ah-MEHN-toh

10) **coperta di lana** (wool blanket)
koh-PEHR-tah dee LAH-na

11) **arrostire marshmallows** (to roast marshmallows)
ahr-roh-STEE-reh marshmallows

12) **decorare il giardino** (to decorate the yard)
deh-koh-RAH-reh eel jee-ahr-DEE-noh

Quest'anno per Halloween ho ricevuto moltissimi dolcetti!
This year for Halloween, I got a lot of candy!

Mi piacerebbe intagliare le zucche insieme.
I would like us to carve pumpkins together.

Adoro l'autunno, ma che fatica raccogliere tutte le foglie in giardino!
I love the autumn, but how exhausting it is to collect all the leaves in the garden!

LE STAGIONI - INVERNO (THE SEASONS – WINTER)

1) **cioccolata calda** (hot chocolate)
   chi-oh-koh-LAH-tah KAHL-dah

2) **slitta** (sled)
   SLEE-tah

3) **muffole** (mittens)
   MOOF-foh-leh

4) **piumino** (puffer jacket)
   pee-oo-MEE-noh

5) **zuppa** (soup)
   DZOO-pah

6) **biscotti allo zenzero** (gingerbread cookies)
   bee-SKO-tee AHL-loh DZEHN-dzeh-roh

7) **finestra ghiacciata** (frosty window)
   fee-NEH-strah ghee-ah-chi-AH-tah

8) **pigna** (pinecone)
   PEE-ñah

9) **pattinaggio sul ghiaccio** (ice skating)
   paht-tee-NAH-jeeoh sool ghee-AH-chi-oh

10) **sci** (ski)
    she

11) **pista di pattinaggio** (ice rink)
    PEE-stah dee pah-tee-NAH-jeeoh

12) **palla di nave** (snowball)
    PAHL-lah dee NEH-veh

L'odore di biscotti allo zenzero appena usciti dal forno è unico.
The smell of gingerbread cookies fresh out of the oven is unique.

Non potrei sopravvivere all'inverno senza il mio piumino!
I could not survive winter without my puffer jacket!

Per cena hanno preparato una bella zuppa calda.
They cooked a nice hot soup for dinner.

TEMPO (TIME)

1) **fuso orario** (time zone)
FOO-soh oh-RAH-reeoh

2) **secondo** (second)
seh-KOHN-doh

3) **minuto** (minute)
mee-NOO-toh

4) **ora** (hour)
OH-rah

5) **giorno** (day)
jee-OHR-noh

6) **settimana** (week)
seh-tee-MAH-nah

7) **due settimane** (fortnight)
DOO-eh seh-tee-MAH-neh

8) **mese** (month)
MEH-seh

9) **anno** (year)
AHN-noh

10) **alba** (dawn)
AHL-bah

11) **mattino/mattina** (morning)
mah-TEE-noh/mah-TEE-nah

12) **mezzogiorno** (noon/midday)
meh-dzoh-JEEOHR-noh

13) **pomeriggio** (afternoon)
poh-meh-REE-jeoh

14) **tramonto** (dusk)
trah-MOHN-toh

15) **notte** (night)
NOH-teh

16) **mezzanotte** (midnight)
meh-dzah-NOH-teh

17) **data** (date)
DAH-tah

18) **calendario** (calendar)
kah-lehn-DAH-reeoh

Puoi uscire con i tuoi amici, ma devi tornare a casa prima di mezzanotte.
You can go out with your friends, but you must come back home before midnight.

Il mio mese preferito è ottobre per via del mio compleanno!
My favorite month is October because of my birthday!

Mi sono svegliato all'alba oggi. Sono stanchissimo.
I woke up at dawn today. I am very tired.

① ② ③ ④ ⑤ TODAY APRIL 10 · MAY 2020 ⑧

2020 ⑥

SUN	MON	TUE	WED	THU	FRI	SAT

⑦

SUN	MON	TUE	WED	THU	FRI	SAT
2	3	4	5	6	7	8
9	10	11	12	13	14	15

2020 ⑨

JAN	FEB	MARCH	APRIL
MAY	JUNE	JULY	AUG
SEPT	OCT	NOV	DEC

⑰ MAY 1

⑱ **APRIL 2020**

SUN	MON	TUE	WED	THU	FRI	SAT

⑩ ⑪ ⑫ ⑬ ⑭ ⑮ ⑯

LA CASA (THE HOUSE)

1) **soffitta** (attic)
sohf-FEET-tah

2) **tetto** (roof)
TEH-toh

3) **soffitto** (ceiling)
sohf-FEET-toh

4) **caminetto** (chimney)
kah-mee-NEHT-toh

5) **muro** (wall)
MOO-roh

6) **balcone** (balcony)
bahl-KOH-neh

7) **portico** (porch)
POHR-tee-koh

8) **finestra** (window)
fee-NEH-strah

9) **persiane** (shutters)
pehr-SEEAH-neh

10) **porta** (door)
POHR-tah

11) **scale** (stairs)
SKAH-leh

12) **ringhiera** (bannister)
reen-ghee-EH-rah

13) **pavimento** (floor)
pah-vee-MEHN-toh

14) **scantinato** (basement)
skahn-tee-NAH-toh

15) **cortile sul retro** (backyard)
kohr-TEE-leh sool REH-troh

16) **garage** (garage)
gah-RAHJ

17) **vialetto** (driveway)
vee-ah-LEHT-toh

18) **staccionata** (fence/picket fence)
stah-chi-oh-NAH-tah

19) **cassetta della posta** (mailbox)
kahs-SEHT-tah DEHL-lah POH-stah

20) **corridoio** (hallway/corridor)
kohr-ree-DOH-eeoh

Non ho una soffitta, ma ho un grande scantinato.
I do not have an attic, but I have a big basement.

Puoi chiudere la finestra per favore? Ho freddo.
Can you close the window, please? I am cold.

Dì alla nonna di fare attenzione quando sale le scale.
Tell Grandma to be careful when going up the stairs.

ELEMENTI DELLA CUCINA (KITCHEN ITEMS)

1) **fornelli** (stove)
fohr-NEH-lee

2) **microonde** (microwave oven)
mee-kroh-OHN-deh

3) **fornetto** (toaster oven)
fohr-NEH-toh

4) **mixer elettrico** (electric mixer)
MIX-ehr eh-LEHT-tree-koh

5) **frullatore** (blender)
frool-lah-TOH-reh

6) **tostapane** (toaster)
toh-stah-PAH-neh

7) **macchinetta per il caffè** (coffee maker)
mah-kee-NEHT-tah pehr eel kahf-FEH

8) **frigorifero** (fridge)
free-goh-REE-feh-roh

9) **dispensa** (pantry)
dee-SPEHN-sah

10) **credenza** (cupboard)
kreh-DEHN-dzah

11) **tortiera** (cake pan)
tohr-tee-EH-rah

12) **padella** (frying pan)
pah-DEHL-lah

13) **pentola** (pot)
PEHN-toh-lah

14) **stampini** (cookie cutters)
stahm-PEE-nee

15) **ciotola** (mixing bowl)
che-OH-toh-lah

16) **scolapasta** (colander)
skoh-lah-PAH-stah

17) **colino** (strainer)
koh-LEE-noh

18) **mattarello** (rolling pin)
maht-tah-REHL-loh

19) **guanto da forno** (oven mitt)
goo-AHN-toh dah FOHR-noh

20) **grembiule** (apron)
grehm-bee-OO-leh

Prima di fare i biscotti metti il grembiule.
Before making cookies, put the apron on.

La dispensa è vuota.
The pantry is empty.

Preferisco cuocere senza burro. È più salutare.
I prefer cooking without butter. It is healthier.

ELEMENTI DELLA CAMERA DA LETTO (BEDROOM ITEMS)

1) **letto** (bed)
LEHT-toh

2) **materasso** (mattress)
mah-teh-RAH-soh

3) **biancheria da letto** (bedding/bed linen)
bee-ahn-keh-REE-ah dah LEHT-toh

4) **cuscino** (pillow)
coo-SHE-noh

5) **lenzuola** (sheet)
lehn-dzoo-OH-lah

6) **coperta** (blanket)
koh-PEHR-tah

7) **copriletto** (spread)
koh-pree-LEHT-toh

8) **federa** (pillowcase)
FEH-deh-rah

9) **comodino** (nightstand)
koh-moh-DEE-noh

10) **orologio da tavolo** (table clock)
oh-roh-LOH-jeoh dah TAH-voh-loh

11) **lampada da tavolo** (table light)
lahm-PAH-dah dah TAH-voh-loh

12) **armadio** (closet)
ahr-MAH-deeoh

13) **sedia a dondolo** (rocking chair)
SEH-dee-ah ah DOHN-doh-loh

14) **abat-jour** (lamp)
ah-BAH joor

15) **specchio** (mirror)
SPEH-key-oh

16) **comò** (dresser)
koh-MOH

17) **tenda** (curtain)
TEHN-dah

18) **culla** (cradle/crib)
COO-lah

19) **giochino** (crib mobile)
jeoh-KEY-noh

20) **appendino** (hanger)
ahp-pehn-DEE-noh

Ho troppo caldo. Leva la coperta.
I am too hot. Take the blanket away.

Non le piacciono più le sue tende gialle.
She does not like her yellow curtains anymore.

Il bebé dorme nella sua culla.
The baby is sleeping in his cradle.

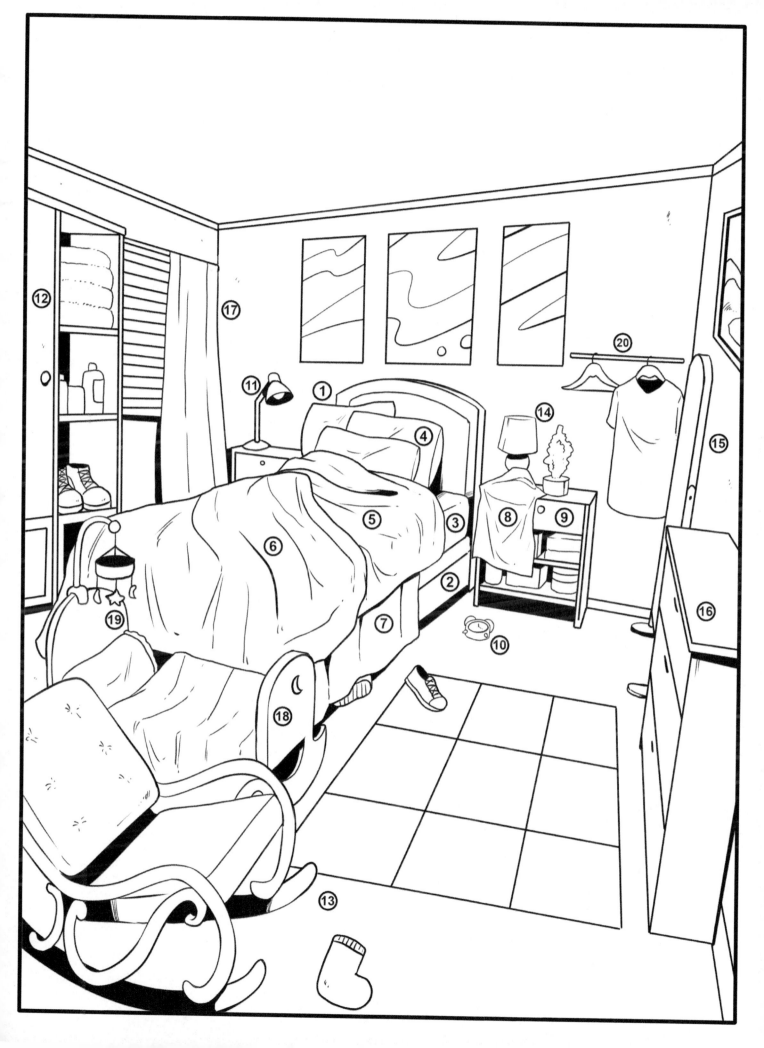

ELEMENTI DEL BAGNO (BATHROOM ITEMS)

1) **tenda della doccia** (shower curtain)
   TEHN-dah DEH-lah DO-chi-ah

2) **asciugamano** (towel)
   ah-she-oo-gah-MAH-noh

3) **portasciugamani** (towel rack)
   pohr-tah-she-oo-gah-MAH-nee

4) **asciugamano per le mani** (hand towel)
   ah-she-oo-gah-MAH-noh pehr leh MAH-nee

5) **vasca da bagno** (bathtub)
   VAH-skah dah BAH-ñoh

6) **doccia** (shower)
   DOH-chi-ah

7) **gabinetto/WC** (toilet/WC)
   gah-bee-NEH-toh/VEE-chi

8) **lavandino** (sink/washbasin)
   lah-vahn-DEE-noh

9) **rubinetto** (faucet/tap)
   roo-bee-NEH-toh

10) **tappetino** (bathmat)
    tah-peh-TEE-noh

11) **armadietto delle medicine** (medicine cabinet)
    ahr-mah-dee-EHT-toh DEH-leh meh-dee-CHI-neh

12) **dentifricio** (toothpaste)
    dehn-tee-FREE-chi-oh

13) **spazzolino da denti** (toothbrush)
    spah-dzoh-LEE-noh dah DEHN-tee

14) **shampoo** (shampoo)
    she-AHM-poh

15) **pettine** (comb)
    PEH-tee-neh

16) **sapone** (soap)
    sah-POH-neh

17) **schiuma da barba** (shaving foam)
    ski-OO-mah dah BAHR-bah

18) **rasoio** (razor/shaver)
    rah-SOH-e-oh

19) **carta igienica** (toilet paper)
    KAHR-tah e-jee-EH-nee-kah

20) **sturalavandini** (plunger)
    stoo-rah-lah-vahn-DEE-nee

21) **scopino** (toilet brush)
    skoh-PEE-noh

22) **cestino** (wastebasket)
    che-STEE-noh

Troverai l'antibiotico nell'armadietto delle medicine.
You will find the antibiotic in the medicine cabinet.

Oggi devo lavare il bagno.
I have to clean the bathroom today.

Hai visto il mio spazzolino da denti?
Have you seen my toothbrush?

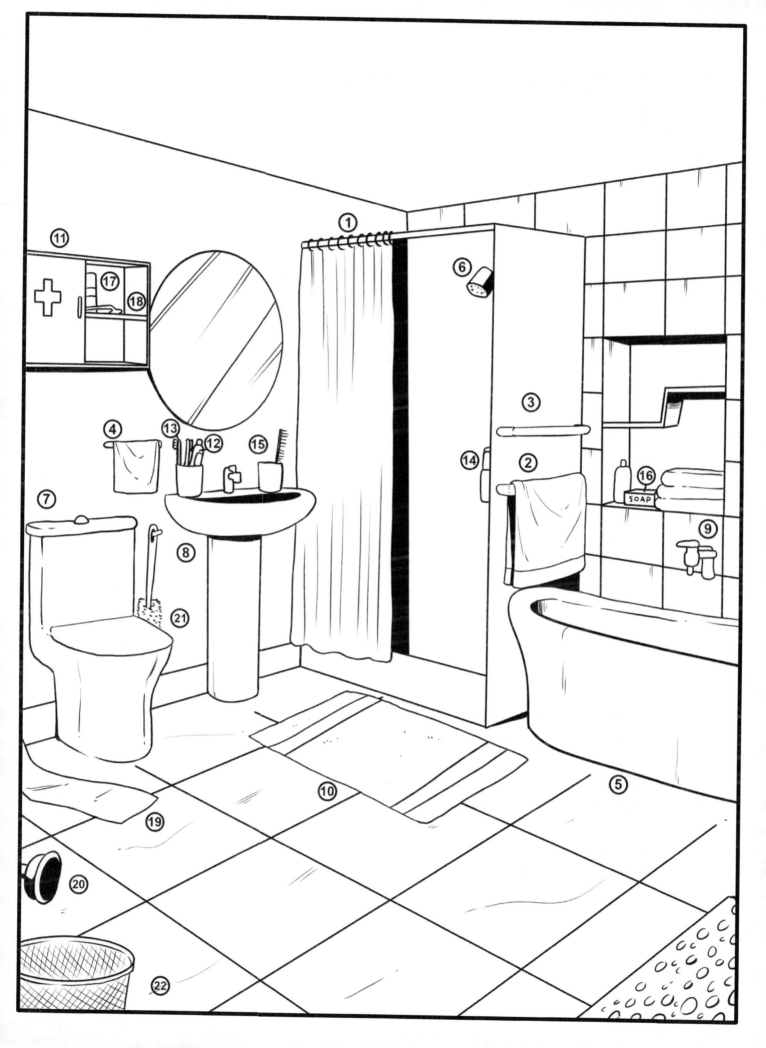

ELEMENTI DEL SALOTTO (LIVING ROOM ITEMS)

1) **arredo** (furniture)
   ahr-REH-doh

2) **sedia** (chair)
   SEH-dee-ah

3) **divano** (sofa)
   dee-VAH-noh

4) **poltrona** (armchair)
   pohl-TROH-nah

5) **cuscino** (cushion)
   coo-SHE-noh

6) **tavolo basso** (coffee table)
   TAH-voh-loh BAHS-soh

7) **posacenere** (ashtray)
   poh-sah-CHE-neh-reh

8) **vaso** (vase)
   VAH-soh

9) **decorazioni** (ornaments)
   deh-koh-rah-DZEOH-nee

10) **libreria** (bookshelf/bookcase)
    lee-breh-REE-ah

11) **portariviste** (magazine holder)
    pohr-tah-ree-VEE-steh

12) **stereo** (stereo)
    STEH-reh-oh

13) **casse** (speakers)
    KAH-seh

14) **caminetto** (fireplace)
    kah-mee-NEH-toh

15) **lampadario** (chandelier)
    lahm-pah-DAH-reeoh

16) **lampada** (lamp)
    LAHM-pah-dah

17) **lampadina** (light bulb)
    lahm-pah-DEE-nah

18) **orologio da parete** (wall clock)
    oh-roh-LOH-jeoh dah pah-REH-teh

19) **dipinto** (painting)
    dee-PEEN-toh

20) **TV/televisione** (TV/television)
    tee-VOO/teh-leh-vee-SEOH-neh

21) **telecomando** (remote control)
    teh-leh-koh-MAHN-doh

22) **console** (video game console)
    kohn-SOHL

I fiori in quel vaso sono bellissimi!
The flowers in that vase are beautiful!

Mi passi il telecomando per favore? Vorrei vedere la partita.
Can you give me the remote control, please? I would like to watch the match.

Il vostro divano è comodissimo. Dove l'avete comprato?
Your sofa is very comfortable. Where did you buy it?

ELEMENTI DELLA SALA DA PRANZO (DINING ROOM ITEMS)

1) **tavolo da pranzo** (dining table)
   TAH-voh-loh dah PRAHN-dzoh

2) **tovaglia** (tablecloth)
   toh-VAH-llah

3) **centrotavola** (centerpiece)
   chen-troh-TAH-voh-lah

4) **tovaglietta** (placemat)
   toh-vah-LLEHT-tah

5) **piatto** (plate)
   pee-AHT-toh

6) **tovagliolo** (napkin)
   toh-vah-LLOH-loh

7) **coltello** (knife)
   kohl-TEHL-loh

8) **forchetta** (fork)
   fohr-KEHT-tah

9) **cucchiaio** (spoon)
   coo-key-AH-eeoh

10) **caraffa** (pitcher/jug)
    kah-RAHF-fah

11) **bicchiere** (glass)
    bee-key-EH-reh

12) **tazza** (mug/cup)
    TAH-dzah

13) **saliera** (saltshaker)
    sahl-ee-EH-rah

14) **pepiera** (pepper shaker)
    peh-pee-EH-rah

15) **vassoio** (tray)
    vahs-SOH-eeoh

16) **bibita** (drink/beverage)
    BEE-bee-tah

17) **cibo** (food)
    CHI-boh

18) **snack** (snack)
    as in English

Il tovagliolo è caduto sul pavimento.
The napkin fell on the floor.

Il tuo bicchiere è ancora mezzo pieno.
Your glass is still half-full.

Vorrei davvero una bibita rinfrescante.
I would really like a refreshing drink.

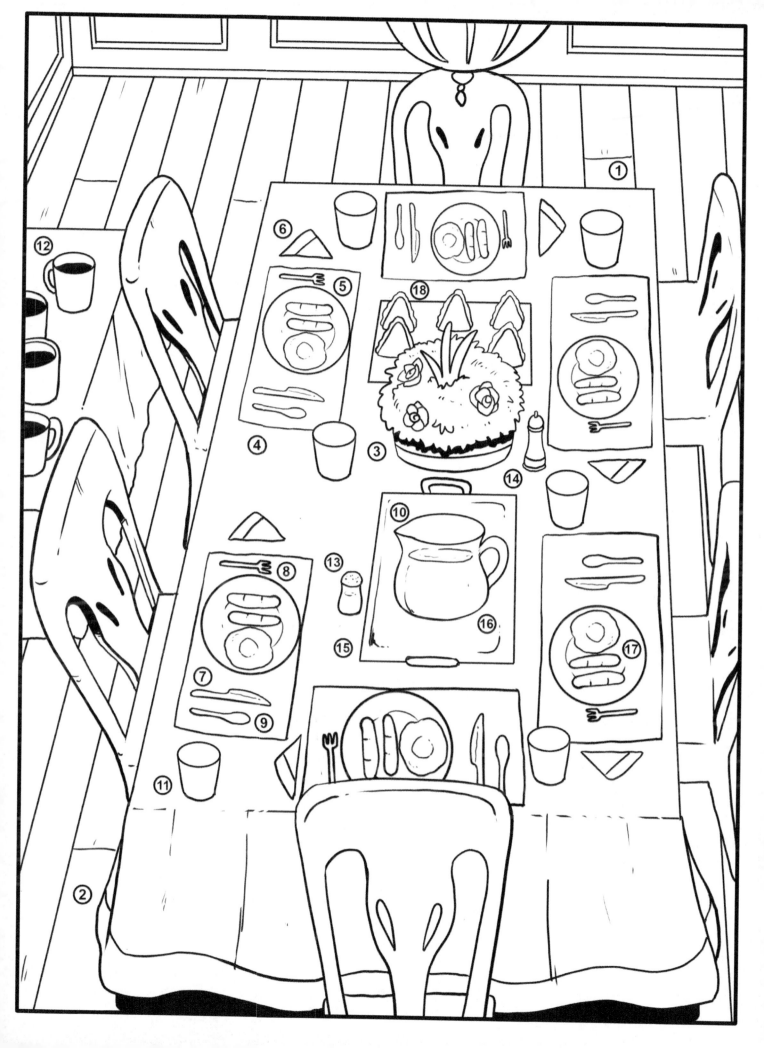

QUIZ #3

Use arrows to match the corresponding translations:

a. window   1. tenda

b. napkin   2. porta

c. oven   3. pattinaggio sul ghiaccio

d. bed   4. finestra

e. toilet paper   5. frigorifero

f. glass   6. forchetta

g. mirror   7. bicchiere

h. curtain   8. letto

i. chair   9. specchio

j. dining table   10. tavolo da pranzo

k. remote control   11. doccia

l. door   12. forno

m. fridge   13. sedia

n. ice skating   14. tovagliolo

o. fork   15. telecomando

p. shower   16. carta igienica

Fill in the blank spaces with the options below (use each word only once):

Benvenuti a casa mia! Non è grande, ma è molto accogliente. Al piano terra c'è la mia stanza preferita, il _____, dove ho la _____ e la _____ che uso per giocare ai miei videogiochi preferiti. Accanto c'è la _____, dove i miei genitori preparano dei piatti ottimi. La _____ è sulla destra; abbiamo un grande _____ che usiamo per mangiare, con una _____ rossa e un _____ con dei fiori bellissimi. Abbiamo sei _____, ma possiamo aggiungerne altre quando abbiamo ospiti. La mia _____ è al piano di sopra. Il mio _____ è molto comodo; visto che è inverno, ho le _____ più pesanti.

camera da letto	cucina
tavolo da pranzo	televisione
lenzuola	tovaglia
console	sala da pranzo
salotto	vaso
sedie	letto

IL GIARDINO (THE GARDEN/THE BACKYARD)

1) **giardiniere** (gardener)
jeahr-dee-nee-EH-reh

2) **capanno** (shed)
kah-PAHN-noh

3) **cespuglio** (bush)
che-SPOO-lloh

4) **prato** (lawn)
PRAH-toh

5) **erba** (grass)
EHR-bah

6) **fiore** (flower)
fee-OH-reh

7) **tubo di irrigazione** (garden hose)
TOO-boh dee eer-ree-gah-DZEOH-neh

8) **annaffiatoio** (watering can)
ah-nahf-fee-ah-TOH-eeoh

9) **vaso da fiori** (flowerpot)
VAH-soh dah fee-OH-ree

10) **guanti da giardino** (gardening gloves)
goo-AHN-tee dah jeahr-DEE-noh

11) **pala** (shovel)
PAH-lah

12) **rastrello** (rake)
rah-STREHL-loh

13) **forca da giardinaggio** (gardening fork)
FOHR-kah dah jeahr-dee-NAH-jeoh

14) **potatrici** (pruners/pruning shears)
poh-tah-TREE-chi

15) **paletta da giardinaggio** (garden trowel)
pah-LEHT-tah dah jeahr-dee-NAH-jeoh

16) **rubinetto** (tap)
roo-bee-NEH-toh

17) **carriola** (wheelbarrow)
kah-ree-OH-lah

18) **tosaerba** (lawn mower)
toh-sah-EHR-bah

19) **lanterna** (lantern)
lahn-TEHR-nah

20) **rampicante** (vine)
rahm-pee-KAHN-teh

Devo tagliare l'erba nel mio giardino. È fuori controllo!
I have to cut the grass in my garden. It has grown out of control!

La carriola è troppo pesante. Mi puoi dare una mano?
The wheelbarrow is too heavy. Could you help me?

Non sa prendersi cura del giardino. È meglio se chiama un giardiniere.
He does not know how to take care of the garden. It may be better to call a gardener.

LA STANZA DEL BUCATO (THE LAUNDRY ROOM)

1) **lavatrice** (washing machine)
lah-vah-TREE-che

2) **asciugatrice** (dryer)
ah-she-oo-gah-TREE-che

3) **ferro da stiro** (iron)
FEHR-roh dah STEE-roh

4) **asse da stiro** (ironing board)
AHS-seh dah STEE-roh

5) **sapone da bucato** (laundry soap)
sah-POH-neh dah boo-KAH-toh

6) **detersivo per il bucato** (laundry detergent)
deh-tehr-SEE-voh pehr eel boo-KAH-toh

7) **ammorbidente** (fabric softener)
ah-mohr-bee-DEHN-teh

8) **cesta del bucato** (laundry basket)
CHE-stah dehl boo-KAH-toh

9) **vestiti sporchi** (dirty clothes)
veh-STEE-tee SPOHR-key

10) **vestiti puliti** (clean laundry)
veh-STEE-tee poo-LEE-tee

11) **scopa** (broom)
SKOH-pah

12) **paletta** (dustpan)
pah-LEH-tah

13) **guanti di gomma** (rubber gloves)
goo-AHN-tee dee GOHM-mah

14) **spugna** (sponge)
SPOO-ñah

15) **vaschetta di plastica** (plastic tub)
vah-SKEHT-tah dee PLAH-stee-kah

16) **mocio** (mop)
MOH-chi-oh

17) **secchio** (bucket)
SEH-key-oh

18) **panni per pulire** (cleaning cloths)
PAHN-nee pehr poo-LEE-reh

19) **spazzola** (scrub brush)
SPAH-dzoh-lah

20) **candeggina** (bleach)
kahn-deh-GEE-nah

21) **disinfettante** (disinfectant)
dee-seen-feht-TAHN-teh

22) **cestino della spazzatura** (garbage can)
che-STEE-noh DEHL-lah spah-dzah-TOO-rah

Sei in punizione! Prendi scopa e paletta e pulisci la tua camera.
You are grounded! Take a broom and a dustpan, and clean your room.

Uso la lavatrice due volte a settimana.
I use the washing machine twice a week.

Abbiamo una montagna di vestiti sporchi da lavare.
We have a mountain of dirty clothes to wash.

LA SCUOLA (THE SCHOOL/THE UNIVERSITY)

1) **insegnante** (teacher)
   een-seh-ÑAHN-teh

2) **studente** (student)
   stoo-DEHN-teh

3) **classe** (classroom)
   KLAH-seh

4) **armadietto** (locker)
   ahr-mah-dee-EHT-toh

5) **bacheca** (bulletin board)
   bah-KEH-kah

6) **foglio di carta** (sheet of paper)
   FOH-lleoh dee KAHR-tah

7) **libro** (book)
   LEE-broh

8) **quaderno** (notebook)
   coo-ah-DEHR-noh

9) **colla** (glue)
   KOHL-lah

10) **forbici** (scissors)
    FOHR-bee-chi

11) **matita** (pencil)
    mah-TEE-tah

12) **gomma** (eraser)
    GOHM-mah

13) **temperamatite** (pencil sharpener)
    tehm-peh-rah-mah-TEE-teh

14) **penna** (pen)
    PEHN-nah

15) **pennarello** (marker)
    pehn-nah-REHL-loh

16) **evidenziatore** (highlighter)
    eh-vee-dehn-dzeah-TOH-reh

17) **busta** (envelope)
    BOO-stah

18) **cartellina** (clipboard)
    kahr-tehl-LEE-nah

19) **lavagna** (blackboard)
    lah-VAH-ñah

20) **calcolatrice** (calculator)
    kahl-koh-lah-TREE-che

21) **righello** (ruler)
    ree-GHEHL-loh

22) **spillatrice** (stapler)
    speel-lah-TREE-che

23) **astuccio** (pouch/pencil case)
    ah-STOO-chi-oh

24) **banco** (school desk)
    BAHN-koh

25) **cattedra** (table)
    KAH-teh-drah

26) **computer** (computer)
    as in English

Ho dimenticato di portare il mio quaderno di Italiano oggi.
I forgot to bring my Italian notebook today.

Devo comprare delle matite per il mio fratellino.
I need to buy some pencils for my little brother.

L'UFFICIO (THE OFFICE)

1) **capo** (boss)
KAH-poh

2) **superiore** (superior)
soo-peh-ree-OH-reh

3) **dipendente** (employee)
dee-pehn-DEHN-teh

4) **presidente** (CEO/president)
preh-see-DEHN-teh

5) **socio in affari** (business partner)
SOH-chi-oh een ahf-FAH-ree

6) **collega** (colleague)
kohl-LEH-gah

7) **collaboratore** (co-worker)
kohl-lah-boh-rah-TOH-reh

8) **segretario** (secretary)
she-greh-TAH-ree-oh

9) **postazione** (cubicle)
poh-stah-DZEOH-neh

10) **sedia girevole** (swivel chair)
SEH-dee-ah gee-REH-voh-leh

11) **scrivania** (desk)
skree-vah-NEE-ah

12) **computer** (computer)
as in English

13) **stampante** (printer)
stahm-PAHN-teh

14) **cancelleria** (office supplies)
kahn-chel-leh-REE-ah

15) **timbro** (rubber stamp)
TEAM-broh

16) **scotch** (tape)
as in English

17) **cartella** (folder)
kahr-TEHL-lah

18) **schedario** (filing cabinet)
skeh-DAH-reoh

19) **fax** (fax)
fahx

20) **telefono** (telephone)
the-LEH-foh-noh

La mia sedia girevole si è rotta. Devo chiederne una nuova.
My swivel chair broke. I have to ask for a new one.

Quanti dipendenti ha la tua azienda?
How many employees does your company have?

Il mio capo è insopportabile!
My boss is intolerable!

PROFESSIONI (PROFESSIONS/OCCUPATIONS)

1) **ingegnere** (engineer)
   een-geh-ÑEH-reh

2) **astronauta** (astronaut)
   ah-stroh-NAH-oo-tah

3) **pilota** (pilot)
   pee-LOH-tah

4) **giudice** (judge)
   gee-OO-dee-che

5) **pompiere** (firefighter)
   pohm-pee-EH-reh

6) **poliziotto** (police officer)
   poh-lee-dzee-OH-toh

7) **chef** (chef)
   as in English

8) **direttore d'orchestra** (conductor)
   dee-reh-TOH-reh dohr-KEH-strah

9) **professore** (professor)
   proh-feh-SOH-reh

10) **ballerina** (dancer)
    bahl-leh-REE-nah

11) **uomo d'affari** (businessman)
    oo-OH-moh dahf-FAH-ree

12) **addestratore** (animal trainer)
    ahd-deh-strah-TOH-reh

Il mio sogno è diventare un astronauta!
My dream is to become an astronaut!

Ha lavorato come ballerina per dieci anni.
She worked as a dancer for ten years.

Un professore deve essere molto paziente.
A professor must be very patient.

MEZZI DI TRASPORTO (MEANS OF TRANSPORT)

1) **bici/bicicletta** (bike/bicycle)
BEE-chi/bee-chi-KLEHT-tah

2) **moto/motocicletta**
(motorcycle/motorbike)
MOH-toh/moh-toh-chi-KLEHT-tah

3) **motoslitta** (snowmobile)
moh-toh-SLEET-tah

4) **macchina/auto** (car/automobile)
MAH-key-nah/AH-oo-toh

5) **bus** (bus)
boos

6) **camion** (truck)
KAH-mee-ohn

7) **metro** (subway)
MEH-troh

8) **treno** (train)
TREH-noh

9) **moto d'acqua** (Jet Ski)
MOH-toh DAH-coo-ah

10) **barca** (boat)
BAHR-kah

11) **crociera** (cruise ship)
kroh-chi-EH-rah

12) **sottomarino** (submarine)
soht-toh-mah-REE-noh

13) **dirigibile** (blimp/Zeppelin)
dee-ree-JEE-bee-leh

14) **mongolfiera** (hot-air balloon)
mohn-gohl-fee-EH-rah

15) **aereo** (plane/airplane)
ah-EH-reh-oh

16) **elicottero** (helicopter/chopper)
eh-lee-KOH-teh-roh

17) **navicella spaziale** (space shuttle)
nah-vee-CHEL-lah spah-DZEAH-leh

Preferisco viaggiare in treno per ragioni ambientali.
I prefer traveling by train for environmental reasons.

Sei mai stato su una mongolfiera?
Have you ever been on a hot-air balloon?

Abbiamo una vecchia auto, ma funziona ancora!
We have an old car, but it still works!

PAESAGGI (LANDSCAPES)

1) **montagna** (mountain)
mohn-TAH-ñah

2) **foresta tropicale** (tropical rainforest)
foh-REH-stah troh-pee-KAH-leh

3) **deserto** (desert)
deh-SEHR-toh

4) **vulcano** (volcano)
wool-KAH-noh

5) **rupe** (cliff)
ROO-peh

6) **spiaggia** (beach)
spee-AH-jeah

7) **foresta** (forest)
foh-REH-stah

8) **grotta** (cave)
GROHT-tah

9) **geyser** (geyser)
as in English

10) **cascata** (waterfall/falls)
kah-SKAH-tah

11) **fiume** (river)
fee-OO-meh

12) **rovine antiche** (ancient ruins)
roh-VEE-neh ahn-TEE-keh

Il mio posto felice? La spiaggia!
My happy place? The beach!

Questa città è un deserto di notte.
This city is a desert at night.

Non entrare nella grotta da solo. Potrebbe essere pericoloso.
Do not go into the cave alone. It might be dangerous.

SPORT I (SPORTS I)

1) **tiro con l'arco** (archery)
TEE-roh kohn LAHR-koh

2) **boxe** (boxing)
box

3) **ciclismo** (cycling)
chi-KLEE-smoh

4) **scherma** (fencing)
SKEHR-mah

5) **calcio** (football/soccer)
KAHL-chi-oh

6) **rugby** (rugby)
RAHG-bee

7) **ping pong** (table tennis/ping-pong)
peen pohng

8) **pallavolo** (volleyball)
pahl-lah-VOH-loh

9) **sollevamento pesi** (weightlifting)
sohl-leh-vah-MEHN-toh PEH-see

10) **pattinaggio** (skating)
paht-tee-NAH-jeoh

11) **sport paraolimpici** (paralympic sports)
spohrt pah-rah-oh-LEEM-pee-chi

12) **baseball** (baseball)
as in English

13) **pallacanestro/basket** (basketball)
pahl-lah-kah-NEH-stroh/basket

Il mio migliore amico è un campione di scherma.
My best friend is a fencing champion.

Non so giocare a calcio, ma mi piace guardarlo alla tv!
I cannot play football, but I like watching it on TV!

Hai paura di farti male quando pattini?
Are you scared of hurting yourself while skating?

SPORT II (SPORTS II)

1) **badminton** (badminton)
as in English

2) **ginnastica** (gymnastics)
jean-NAH-stee-kah

3) **canottaggio** (rowing)
kah-noht-TAH-jeoh

4) **arrampicata** (climbing)
ahr-rahm-pee-KAH-tah

5) **surf** (surfing)
sehrf

6) **tennis** (tennis)
TEHN-nees

7) **tappeto elastico** (trampoline)
tahp-PEH-toh eh-LAH-stee-koh

8) **wrestling** (wrestling)
as in English

9) **sci** (skiing)
she

10) **skeleton** (skeleton)
as in English

11) **pattinaggio artistico** (figure skating)
paht-tee-NAH-jeoh ahr-TEE-stee-koh

12) **nuoto** (swimming)
noo-OH-toh

13) **pallanuoto** (water polo)
pahl-lah-noo-OH-toh

14) **hockey** (hockey)
OH-keh-y

Mi piacerebbe imparare a giocare a tennis.
I would like to learn how to play tennis.

Il badminton non è uno sport comune in Italia.
Badminton is not a common sport in Italy.

Se ti senti avventuroso, prova l'arrampicata libera!
If you are feeling adventurous, try free climbing!

IL GIORNO DI NATALE (CHRISTMAS DAY)

1) **vischio** (mistletoe)
VEE-skeoh

2) **ghirlanda** (garland)
gheer-LAHN-dah

3) **albero di Natale** (Christmas tree)
AHL-beh-roh dee nah-TAH-leh

4) **decorazioni natalizie** (Christmas decorations)
deh-koh-rah-DZEOH-nee nah-tah-LEE-dzee-eh

5) **regali di Natale** (Christmas gifts/presents)
reh-GAH-lee dee nah-TAH-leh

6) **cena di Natale** (Christmas dinner)
CHE-nah dee nah-TAH-leh

7) **bastoncino di zucchero** (candy cane)
bah-stohn-CHI-noh dee DZOO-keh-roh

8) **omino di zenzero** (gingerbread man)
oh-MEE-noh dee DZEHN-dzeh-roh

9) **elfo di Natale** (Christmas elf)
EHL-foh dee nah-TAH-leh

10) **cappello di Natale** (Christmas hat)
kahp-PEHL-loh dee nah-TAH-leh

11) **Babbo Natale** (Santa Claus)
BAHB-boh nah-TAH-leh

12) **slitta di Babbo Natale** (Santa's sleigh)
SLEET-tah dee BAHB-boh nah-TAH-leh

13) **stella di Natale** (Christmas star)
STEHL-lah dee nah-TAH-leh

14) **pupazzo di neve** (snowman)
poo-PAH-dzoh dee NEH-veh

15) **candele** (candles)
kahn-DEH-leh

Adoro quando la casa è piena di decorazioni natalizie!
I love when the house is filled with Christmas decorations!

Puoi accendere le candele accanto al camino?
Could you light the candles next to the fireplace?

I bambini hanno fatto un pupazzo di neve in giardino.
The children made a snowman in the garden.

QUIZ #4

Use arrows to match the corresponding translations:

a. Christmas tree	1. rupe
b. boxing	2. fiume
c. washing machine	3. crociera
d. Christmas decorations	4. pala
e. gardener	5. regalo
f. cruise ship	6. aereo
g. engineer	7. boxe
h. river	8. banco
i. plane	9. decorazioni natalizie
j. cliff	10. insegnante
k. shovel	11. asciugatrice
l. present/gift	12. albero di Natale
m. volleyball	13. lavatrice
n. teacher	14. pallavolo
o. desk	15. ingegnere
p. dryer	16. giardiniere

Fill in the blank spaces with the options below (use each word only once):

Lavoro come _____ in una _____ media. Adoro la mia _____ perché mi permette di condividere le cose che so con i miei _____. Adesso è _____, quindi non c'è scuola e i ragazzi sono in vacanza. Dobbiamo ancora comprare tutti i _____ e le _____ per la tavola!

Nel mio tempo libero, mi piace giocare a _____ e a _____. Anche i miei figli fanno sport; loro fanno _____ due volte alla settimana. Visto che adesso sono liberi, mi aiutano a mettere le _____ in tutta la casa e a preparare gli _____!

Natale   scuola

pallacanestro   omini di zenzero

insegnante   decorazioni natalizie

candele   studenti

boxe   pallavolo

professione   regali

STRUMENTI MUSICALI (MUSICAL INSTRUMENTS)

1) **chitarra acustica** (acoustic guitar)
kih-TAHR-rah ah-COO-stee-kah

2) **chitarra elettrica** (electric guitar)
kih-TAHR-rah eh-LEHT-tree-kah

3) **basso** (bass guitar)
BAHS-soh

4) **batteria** (drums)
baht-teh-REE-ah

5) **piano** (piano)
pee-AH-noh

6) **trombetta** (trumpet)
trohm-BEHT-tah

7) **armonica** (harmonica)
ahr-MOH-nee-kah

8) **flauto** (flute)
FLAH-oo-toh

9) **clarinetto** (clarinet)
klah-ree-NEHT-toh

10) **arpa** (harp)
AHR-pah

11) **cornamusa** (bagpipe)
kohr-nah-MOO-sah

12) **violoncello** (cello)
vee-oh-lohn-CHEL-loh

13) **violino** (violin)
vee-oh-LEE-noh

14) **sassofono** (saxophone)
sahs-SOH-foh-noh

Vorrei suonare la batteria, ma sono sicuro che i vicini si lamenterebbero.
I would like to play the drums, but I am sure the neighbors would complain.

Ha suonato il piano per dieci anni.
He played the piano for ten years.

Secondo me, lo strumento musicale più elegante è l'arpa.
In my opinion, the most elegant musical instrument is the harp.

FRUTTA (FRUITS)

1) **fragola** (strawberry)
FRAH-goh-lah

2) **papaya** (papaya)
pah-PAH-eeah

3) **prugna** (plum)
PROO-ñah

4) **melone** (melon)
meh-LOH-neh

5) **anguria** (watermelon)
ahn-GOO-ree-ah

6) **banana** (banana)
bah-NAH-nah

7) **mango** (mango)
MAHN-goh

8) **pesca** (peach)
PEH-skah

9) **lampone** (raspberry)
lahm-POH-neh

10) **arancia** (orange)
ah-RAHN-chi-ah

11) **limone** (lemon)
lee-MOH-neh

12) **ananas** (pineapple)
AH-nah-nahs

13) **lime** (lime)
as in English

14) **uva** (grapes)
OO-vah

15) **ciliegia** (cherry)
chi-lee-EH-jeah

16) **mela** (apple)
MEH-lah

17) **pera** (pear)
PEH-rah

18) **pompelmo** (grapefruit)
pohm-PEHL-moh

19) **guanabana** (soursop)
goo-ah-nah-BAH-nah

20) **cocco** (coconut)
KOH-koh

Mi piacciono le arance, ma odio le mele!
I like oranges, but I hate apples!

Al supermercato non c'erano più lamponi.
At the supermarket there were no more raspberries.

I limoni sono troppo aspri.
Lemons are too sour.

VERDURE (VEGETABLES)

1) **cavolfiore** (cauliflower)
   kah-vohl-fee-OH-reh

2) **asparago** (asparagus)
   ah-SPAH-rah-goh

3) **broccolo** (broccoli)
   BROH-koh-loh

4) **cavolo** (cabbage)
   KAH-voh-loh

5) **carciofo** (artichoke)
   kahr-chi-OH-foh

6) **cavoletti di Bruxelles** (Brussels
   sprouts)
   kah-voh-LEHT-tee dee broo-XEHL

7) **mais** (corn)
   MAH-ees

8) **lattuga** (lettuce)
   laht-TOO-gah

9) **spinaci** (spinach)
   spee-NAH-chi

10) **pomodoro** (tomato)
    poh-moh-DOH-roh

11) **cetrioli** (cucumbers)
    che-tree-OH-lee

12) **zucchine** (zucchini)
    dzoo-KIH-neh

13) **funghi** (mushrooms)
    FOON-ghee

14) **rucola** (arugula)
    ROO-koh-lah

15) **melanzana** (eggplant)
    meh-lahn-DZAH-nah

16) **peperone** (bell pepper)
    peh-peh-ROH-neh

17) **cipolla** (onion)
    chi-POH-lah

18) **zucca** (pumpkin)
    DZOO-kah

19) **patata** (potato)
    pah-TAH-tah

20) **bietola** (Swiss chard)
    bee-EH-toh-lah

Per me senza cipolle, grazie.
Without onions for me, please.

Un'ottima insalata con rucola e pomodori.
A delicious salad with arugula and tomatoes.

Non mi piace per niente il cavolfiore.
I do not like cauliflower at all.

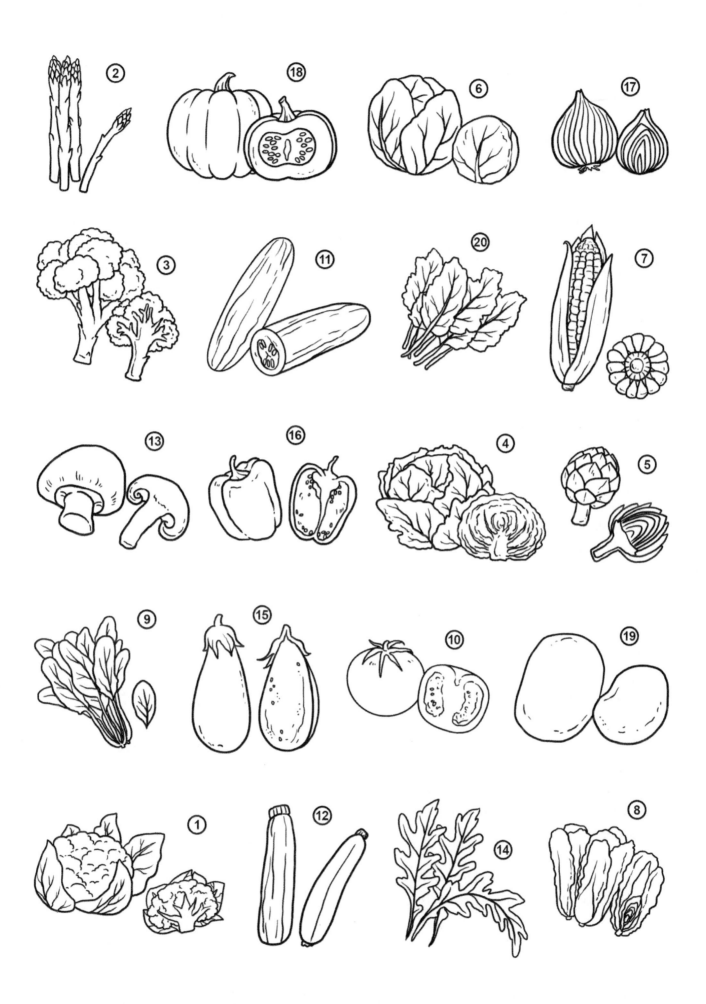

TECNOLOGIA (TECHNOLOGY)

1) **cellulare** (mobile / cell phone)
   che-loo-LAH-reh

2) **dispositivo** (device)
   dee-spoh-see-TEE-voh

3) **computer** (computer)
   as in English

4) **web cam** (web cam)
   WEB kahm

5) **chiavetta USB** (flash drive)
   kih-ah-VEHT-tah oo-EHS-seh BEE

6) **disco rigido** (hard drive)
   DEE-skoh REE-jee-doh

7) **scheda di memoria** (memory card)
   SKEH-dah dee meh-MOH-ree-ah

8) **lettore di schede** (card reader)
   leht-TOH-reh dee SKEH-deh

9) **wireless** (wireless)
   as in English

10) **pannello solare** (solar panel)
    pahn-NEHL-loh soh-LAH-reh

11) **stampante** (printer)
    stahm-PAHN-teh

12) **scanner** (scanner)
    SKAHN-nehr

Usiamo solo pannelli solari.
We use solar panels only.

Posso venire a casa tua per usare la stampante?
May I come over to use your printer?

Ho scaricato tutti i file sulla chiavetta USB.
I downloaded all the files on the flash drive.

SCIENZA (SCIENCE)

1) **laboratorio** (laboratory)
   lah-boh-rah-TOH-reoh

2) **ricercatore** (researcher)
   ree-cher-kah-TOH-reh

3) **calcoli** (calculations)
   KAHL-koh-lee

4) **scienziato** (scientist)
   she-ehn-DZEAH-toh

5) **camice da laboratorio** (lab coat)
   KAH-mee-che dah lah-boh-rah-TOH-ree-oh

6) **esperimento** (experiment)
   eh-speh-ree-MEHN-toh

7) **dispositivi di protezione individuale** (personal protective equipment)
   dee-spoh-see-TEE-vee dee proh-teh-DZEOH-neh een-dee-vee-doo-AH-leh

8) **test** (test)
   as in Eglish

9) **premio** (prize)
   PREH-meoh

10) **rischio** (risk)
    REE-skeoh

11) **strumento** (instrument)
    stroo-MEHN-toh

12) **statistiche** (statistics)
    stah-TEE-stee-keh

Il nostro esperimento è durato tutta la giornata.
Our experiment lasted all day long.

Spero di vincere un premio per la mia ricerca!
I hope I win a prize for my research!

C'è sempre un rischio quando si lavora sui test.
There is always a risk when you work on tests.

ASTRONOMIA (ASTRONOMY)

1) **telescopio** (telescope)
   teh-leh-SKOH-pee-oh

2) **sole** (sun)
   SOH-leh

3) **luna** (moon)
   LOO-nah

4) **galassia** (galaxy)
   gah-LAH-see-ah

5) **cintura degli asteroidi** (asteroid belt)
   chin-TOO-rah DEH-llee ah-steh-ROH-ee-dee

6) **buco nero** (black hole)
   BOO-koh NEH-roh

7) **eclisse** (eclipse)
   eh-KLEES-seh

8) **stella cadente** (shooting star)
   STEHL-lah kah-DEHN-teh

9) **stazione spaziale** (space station)
   stah-DZEOH-neh spah-DZEAH-leh

10) **nana bianca** (white dwarf)
    NAH-nah bee-AHN-kah

11) **gigante rossa** (red giant)
    jee-GAHN-teh ROHS-sah

12) **orbita** (orbit)
    OHR-beet-ah

13) **costellazione** (constellation)
    koh-stehl-lah-DZEOH-neh

14) **energia oscura** (dark energy)
    eh-nehr-JEAH oh-SKOO-rah

15) **Plutone** (Pluto)
    ploo-TOH-neh

16) **nebulosa** (nebula)
    neh-boo-LOH-sah

17) **Mercurio** (Mercury)
    mehr-COO-ree-oh

18) **Venere** (Venus)
    VEH-neh-reh

19) **Terra** (Earth)
    TEHR-rah

20) **Marte** (Mars)
    MAHR-teh

21) **Giove** (Jupiter)
    JEOH-veh

22) **Saturno** (Saturn)
    sah-TOOR-noh

23) **Urano** (Uranus)
    oo-RAH-noh

24) **Nettuno** (Neptune)
    neht-TOO-noh

Come regalo di Natale vorrei un telescopio!
I would like a telescope as a Christmas gift!

Guarda la luna stanotte!
Look at the moon tonight!

Giove è il pianeta più grande del sistema solare.
Jupiter is the biggest planet of the solar system.

116

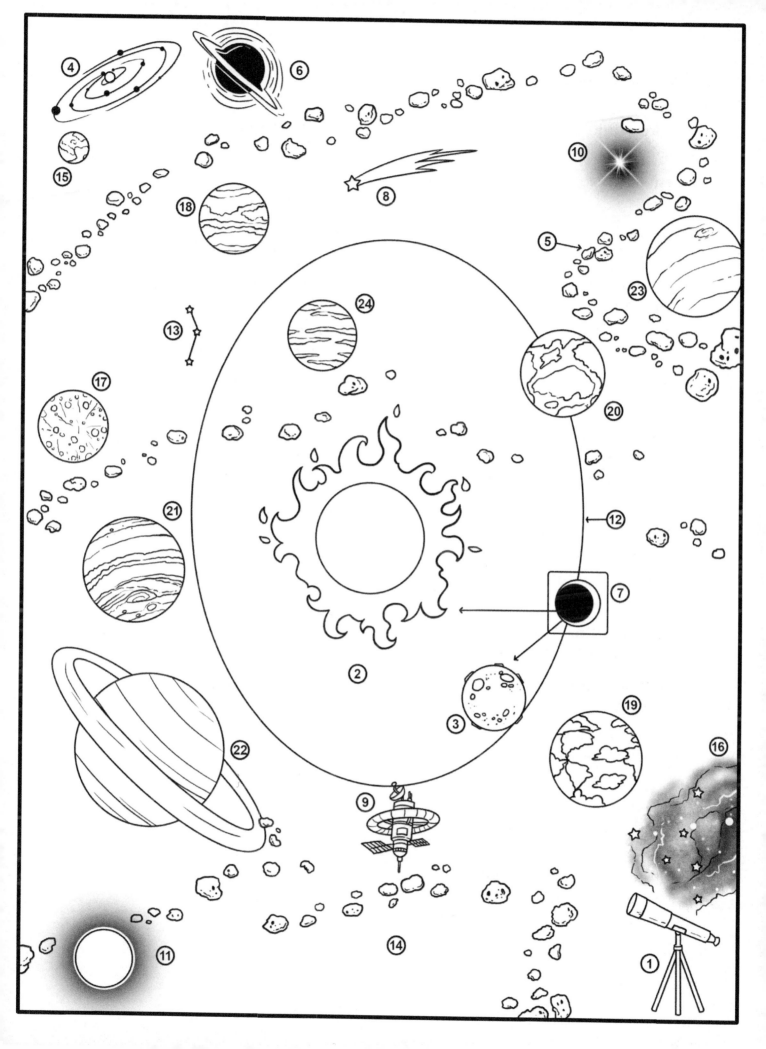

GEOGRAFIA (GEOGRAPHY)

1) **nord** (north)
   nohrd

2) **est** (east)
   ehst

3) **sud** (south)
   sood

4) **ovest** (west)
   oh-vehst

5) **Equatore** (Equator)
   eh-coo-ah-TOH-reh

6) **Tropico del Cancro** (Tropic of Cancer)
   TROH-pee-koh dehl KAHN-kroh

7) **Tropico del Capricorno** (Tropic of Capricorn)
   TROH-pee-koh dehl kah-pree-KOHR-noh

8) **Polo Sud** (South Pole)
   POH-loh sood

9) **Polo Nord** (North Pole)
   POH-loh nohrd

10) **Circolo Artico** (Arctic Circle)
    CHIR-koh-loh AHR-tee-koh

11) **continente** (continent)
    kohn-tee-NEHN-teh

12) **oltreoceano** (overseas)
    ohl-treh-oh-CHE-ah-noh

13) **Africa** (Africa)
    AH-free-kah

14) **Asia** (Asia)
    AH-sea-ah

15) **America del Nord** (North America)
    ah-MEH-ree-kah dehl nohrd

16) **America Centrale** (Central America)
    ah-MEH-ree-kah chen-TRAH-leh

17) **America del Sud** (South América)
    ah-MEH-ree-kah dehl sood

18) **Europa** (Europe)
    eh-oo-ROH-pah

19) **Oceania** (Oceania)
    oh-che-AH-nee-ah

20) **Antartico** (Antarctica)
    ahn-TAHR-tee-kah

21) **meridiano** (meridian)
    meh-ree-dee-AH-noh

22) **parallelo** (parallel)
    pah-rahl-LEH-loh

23) **Oceano Atlantico** (Atlantic Ocean)
    oh-CHE-ah-noh ah-TLAHN-tee-koh

24) **Oceano Pacifico** (Pacific Ocean)
    oh-CHE-ah-noh pah-CHI-fee-koh

Babbo Natale vive al Polo Nord!
Santa Claus lives at the North Pole!

Sei mai stato in America del Sud?
Have you ever been to South America?

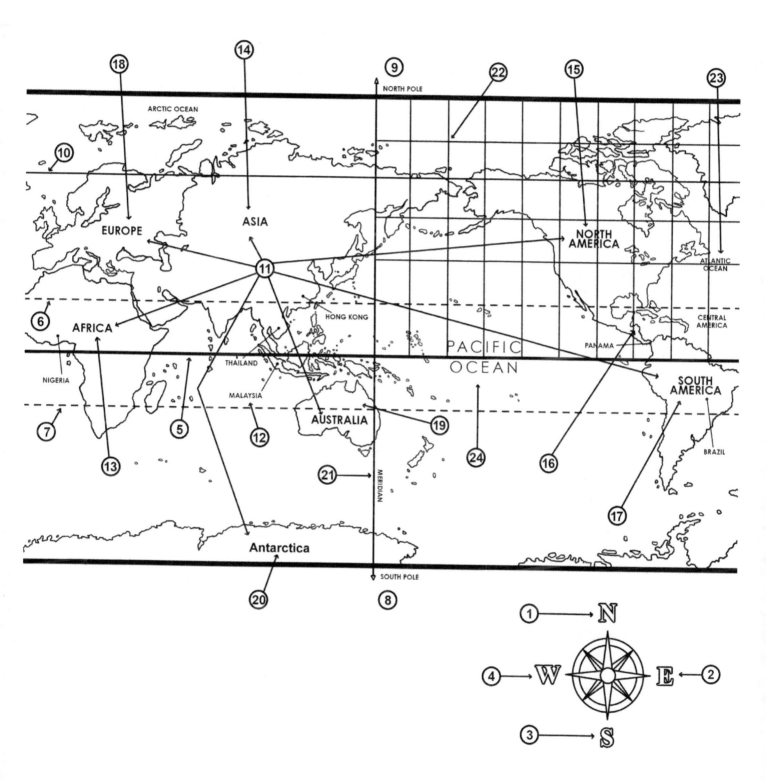

L'OSPEDALE (THE HOSPITAL)

1) **dottore/medico** (doctor/medic)
doht-TOH-reh/MEH-dee-koh

2) **infermiere** (nurse)
een-fehr-mee-EH-reh

3) **ambulanza** (ambulance)
ahm-boo-LAHN-dzah

4) **kit di primo soccorso** (first-aid kit)
keet dee PREE-moh soh-KOHR-soh

5) **termometro** (thermometer)
tehr-MOH-meh-troh

6) **barella** (stretcher)
bah-REHL-lah

7) **siringa** (syringe)
sea-REEN-gah

8) **ago** (needle)
AH-goh

9) **stetoscopio** (stethoscope)
steh-toh-SKOH-pee-oh

10) **stampelle** (crutches)
stahm-PEHL-leh

11) **sedia a rotelle** (wheelchair)
SEH-dee-ah ah roh-TEHL-leh

12) **sala di osservazione** (observation room)
SAH-lah dee ohs-sehr-vah-DZEOH-neh

13) **letto d'ospedale** (hospital bed)
LEHT-toh doh-speh-DAH-leh

14) **iniezione** (injection)
ee-nee-eh-DZEOH-neh

15) **operazione** (surgery)
oh-peh-rah-DZEOH-neh

16) **anamnesi** (medical history)
ah-NAHM-neh-sea

17) **paziente** (patient)
pah-dzee-EHN-teh

18) **pillola** (pill/tablet)
PEEL-loh-lah

Mi sono rotto una gamba; devo usare le stampelle per un mese.
I broke my leg; now I have to use crutches for a month.

Ho la fobia degli aghi!
I have a phobia of needles!

Dove tenete il kit di primo soccorso?
Where do you keep your first-aid kit?

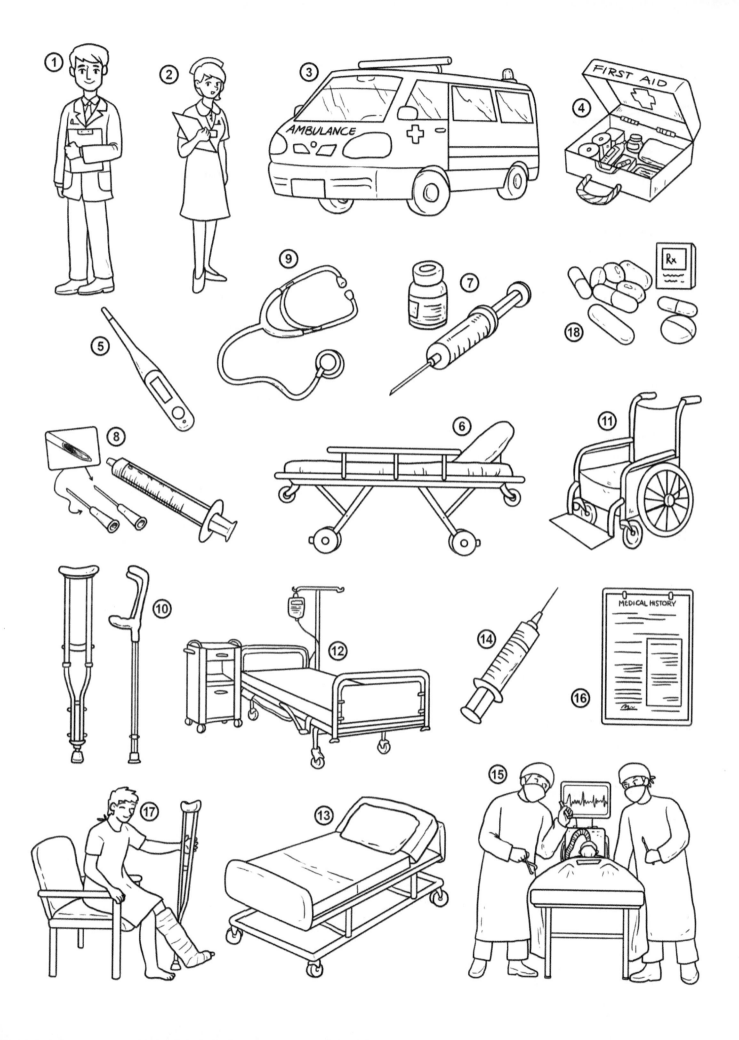

LA FATTORIA (THE FARM)

1) **fienile** (barn)
   phee-eh-NEE-leh

2) **stalla** (cowshed/stable)
   STAHL-lah

3) **contadino** (farmer)
   kohn-tah-DEE-noh

4) **aratro** (plow)
   ah-RAH-troh

5) **silo** (silo)
   SEA-lohs

6) **mulino** (mill)
   moo-LEE-noh

7) **abbeveratoio** (water trough)
   ah-beh-veh-rah-TOH-ee-oh

8) **pollaio** (henhouse)
   pohl-LAH-ee-oh

9) **alveare** (beehive)
   ahl-veh-AH-reh

10) **balla di fieno** (hay bale)
    BAHL-lah dee phee-EH-noh

11) **bovini** (cattle)
    boh-VEE-nee

12) **mungere** (to milk)
    MOON-geh-reh

13) **gregge** (herd/flock)
    GREH-geh

14) **gallina** (hen)
    gahl-LEE-nah

15) **pozzo** (well)
    POH-dzoh

16) **sistema di irrigazione** (irrigation system)
    see-STEH-mah dee eer-ree-gah-DZEOH-neh

17) **spaventapasseri** (scarecrow)
    spah-vehn-tah-PAHS-seh-ree

18) **strada sterrata** (dirt road)
    STRAH-dah stehr-RAH-tah

Il contadino è nella stalla.
The farmer is in the stable.

Puoi prendere l'acqua dal pozzo.
You can take water from the well.

Quante galline avete?
How many hens do you have?

QUIZ #5

Use arrows to match the corresponding translations:

a. cattle

b. device

c. needle

d. hospital

e. drums

f. arugula

g. apple

h. printer

i. to milk

j. researcher

k. hard drive

l. nurse

m. guitar

n. watermelon

o. cauliflower

p. parallels

1. batteria

2. mela

3. bovini

4. infermiere

5. anguria

6. disco rigido

7. cavolfiore

8. dispositivo

9. ricercatore

10. stampante

11. chitarra

12. ago

13. paralleli

14. mungere

15. ospedale

16. rucola

Fill in the blank spaces with the options below (use each word only once):

Cosa mi piace fare nel mio tempo libero? Tantissime cose! Suono il _____ da quando avevo sei anni, e l'_____ da un paio di anni. Lavoro come _____, quindi non ho molto tempo, ma cerco sempre di _____ almeno due volte alla settimana. Per lavoro viaggio molto; il mese scorso ero in Argentina, in _____, e la prossima settimana dovrò andare in _____, in Cina. Un'altra cosa che mi piace fare è mangiare! Amo la _____, in particolare le _____ e i _____, ma sono allergico alle _____. Per quanto riguarda la frutta, la mia preferita sono le _____, ma non mi piace il _____.

America del Sud	verdura
piano	suonare
ciliegie	cipolle
cetrioli	arpa
scienziato	melone
melanzane	Asia

CIBO (FOOD)

1) **uvetta** (raisin)
oo-VEHT-tah

2) **noci** (nuts)
NOH-chi

3) **carne** (meat)
KAHR-neh

4) **agnello** (lamb)
ah-ÑEHL-loh

5) **pesce** (fish)
PEH-sche

6) **pollo** (chicken)
POHL-loh

7) **tacchino** (turkey)
tah-KEE-noh

8) **miele** (honey)
mee-EH-leh

9) **zucchero** (sugar)
DZOO-keh-roh

10) **sale** (salt)
SAH-leh

11) **pepe** (pepper)
PEH-peh

12) **bacon** (bacon)
BEH-kohn

13) **salsicce** (sausages)
sahl-SEA-che

14) **ketchup** (ketchup)
KEH-chap

15) **maionese** (mayonnaise)
mah-ee-oh-NEH-seh

16) **mostarda** (mustard)
moh-STAHR-dah

17) **marmellata** (jam)
mahr-mehl-LAH-tah

18) **burro** (butter)
BOOR-roh

19) **succo** (juice)
SOO-koh

20) **latte** (milk)
LAHT-teh

Ho fatto colazione con pane, burro e marmellata.
I had breakfast with bread, butter and jam.

Preferisci ketchup o maionese nel tuo panino?
Do you prefer ketchup or mayonnaise in your sandwich?

Bevo il latte solo se freddo.
I drink milk only when it is cold.

PIATTI (DISHES)

1) **lasagna** (lasagna)
lah-SAH-ñah

2) **frittata con le patate** (potato omelette)
freet-TAH-tah kohn leh pah-TAH-teh

3) **polpettone** (meatloaf)
pohl-peht-TOH-neh

4) **spaghetti fritti** (fried noodles)
spah-GHET-tee FREET-tee

5) **maccheroni e formaggio** (macaroni and cheese)
mah-keh-ROH-nee eh fohr-MAH-jeoh

6) **paella** (paella)
pah-EH-llah

7) **costolette alla griglia** (barbecue ribs)
koh-stoh-LEHT-teh AHL-lah GREE-llah

8) **pane di mais** (cornbread)
PAH-neh dee MAH-ees

9) **involtini primavera** (spring rolls)
een-vohl-TEE-nee pree-mah-VEH-rah

10) **cheeseburger** (cheeseburger)
chis-BOOR-ghehr

11) **pollo fritto** (fried chicken)
POHL-loh FREET-toh

12) **insalata Ceasar** (Caesar salad)
een-sah-LAH-tah caesar

13) **zuppa di cipolle** (onion soup)
DZOOP-pah dee chi-POHL-leh

14) **insalata di cavolo** (coleslaw)
een-sah-LAH-tah dee KAH-voh-loh

15) **alette di pollo piccanti** (spicy chicken wings)
ah-LEHT-teh dee POHL-loh pee-KAHN-tee

16) **biscotti con gocce di cioccolato** (chocolate chip cookies)
bee-SKOHT-tee kohn GOH-che dee cho-koh-LAH-toh

17) **torta al limone** (key lime pie)
TOHR-tah ahl lee-MOH-neh

18) **cheesecake** (cheesecake)
as in English

Il mio piatto spagnolo preferito è la paella.
My favorite Spanish dish is paella.

Non mi piace la zuppa di cipolle.
I do not like the onion soup.

Non puoi dire di no al cheesecake!
You cannot say no to cheesecake!

FRUTTI DI MARE (SEAFOOD)

1) **acciuga** (anchovy)
   ah-CHOO-gah

2) **merluzzo** (cod)
   mehr-LOO-dzoh

3) **grinceola** (spider crab)
   green-CHE-oh-lah

4) **sgombro** (mackerel)
   SGOHM-broh

5) **aragosta** (lobster)
   ah-rah-GOH-stah

6) **capasanta** (scallop)
   kah-pah-SAHN-tah

7) **dentice** (snapper)
   DEHN-tee-che

8) **uova di salmone** (salmon roe)
   oo-OH-vah dee sahl-MOH-neh

9) **granchio** (crab)
   GRAHN-key-oh

10) **molluschi** (shellfish)
    mohl-LOO-ski

11) **anguilla** (eel)
    ahn-goo-EEL-lah

12) **gambero** (shrimp)
    GAHM-beh-roh

Vi piace lo sgombro?
Do you like mackerel?

I granchi si nascondono negli scogli.
Crabs hide in the rocks.

L'aragosta è molto costosa in Italia.
Lobsters are very expensive in Italy.

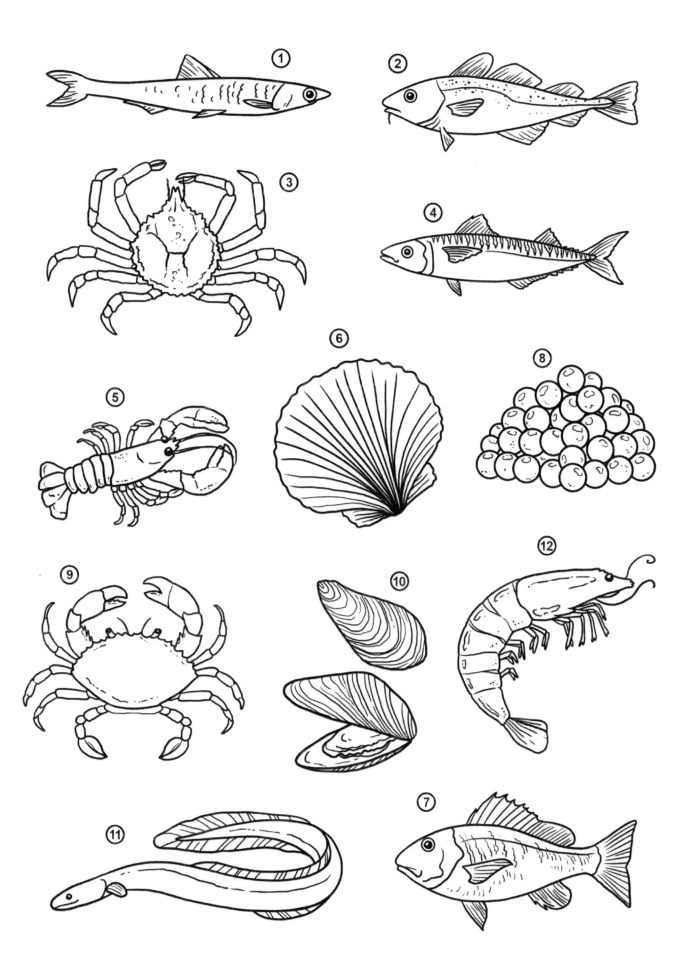

FORME (SHAPES)

1) **cerchio** (circle)
CHER-key-oh

2) **ovale** (oval)
oh-VAH-leh

3) **triangolo** (triangle)
tree-AHN-goh-loh

4) **rettangolo** (rectangle)
reht-TAHN-goh-loh

5) **quadrato** (square)
coo-ah-DRAH-toh

6) **trapezio** (trapezoid)
trah-PEH-dzeoh

7) **rombo** (rhombus)
ROHM-boh

8) **cubo** (cube)
COO-boh

9) **pentagono** (pentagon)
pehn-TAH-goh-noh

10) **esagono** (hexagon)
eh-SAH-goh-noh

11) **freccia** (arrow)
FREH-chi-ah

12) **croce** (cross)
CRAW-che

13) **cuore** (heart)
coo-OH-reh

14) **stella** (star)
STEHL-lah

15) **cilindro** (cylinder)
chi-LEEN-droh

16) **cono** (cone)
KOH-noh

17) **piramide** (pyramid)
pee-RAH-mee-deh

18) **sfera** (sphere)
SPHEH-rah

19) **prisma** (prism)
PREE-smah

Prova a disegnare un triangolo dentro un quadrato.
Try to draw a triangle inside a square.

Il biglietto è a forma di cuore.
The card is heart-shaped.

Un esagono ha sei lati.
A hexagon has six sides.

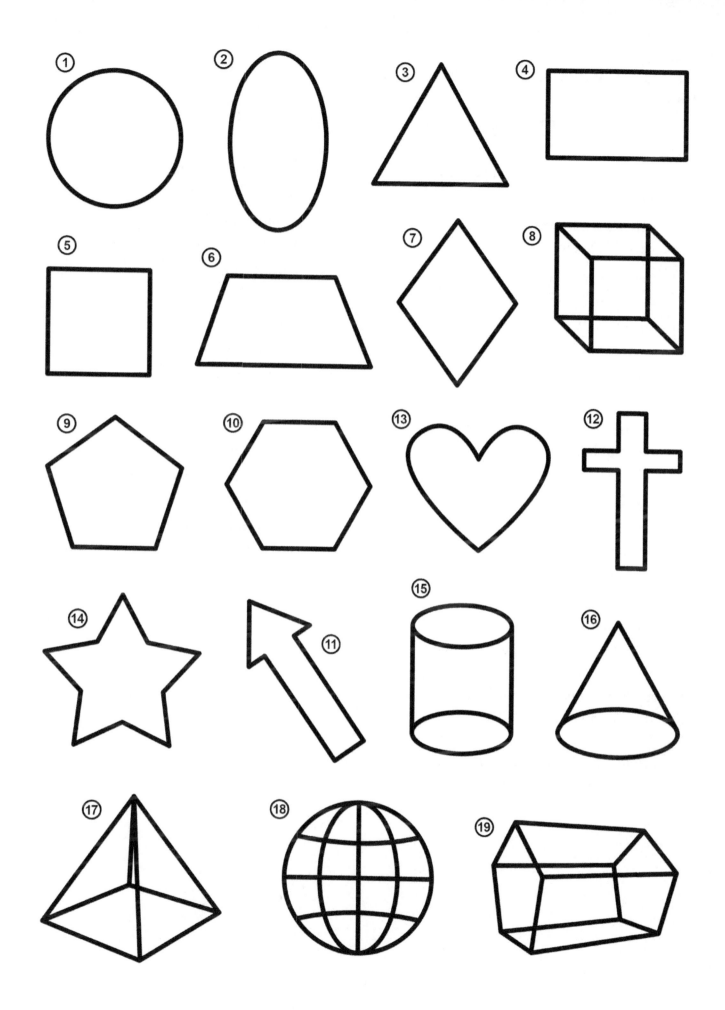

IL SUPERMERCATO (THE SUPERMARKET)

1) **carrello** (shopping cart)
kahr-REHL-loh

2) **espositore** (cabinet/display case)
eh-spoh-sea-TOH-reh

3) **cliente** (customer)
klee-EHN-teh

4) **cassiere** (cashier)
kah-sea-EH-reh

5) **scontrino** (receipt)
skohn-TREE-noh

6) **forno** (bakery)
FOHR-noh

7) **frutta e verdura** (fruits and vegetables)
FROOT-tah eh vehr-DOO-rah

8) **carne** (meat)
KAHR-neh

9) **latticini** (dairy products)
laht-tee-CHI-nee

10) **pesce** (fish)
PEH-sche

11) **surgelati** (frozen food)
soor-jeh-LAH-tee

12) **pollame** (poultry)
pohl-LAH-meh

13) **legumi** (pulses)
leh-GOO-mee

14) **snack** (snacks)
as in English

15) **dolci** (dessert)
DOHL-chi

16) **bibite** (drinks)
BEE-bee-teh

17) **prodotti per la casa** (household items)
proh-DOH-tee pehr lah KAH-sah

18) **nastro trasportatore** (conveyor belt)
NAH-stroh trah-spohr-tah-TOH-reh

Dov'è il reparto frutta e verdura?
Where is the fruit and vegetables aisle?

Lo scontrino è obbligatorio in Italia.
Receipts are mandatory in Italy.

Passiamo a prendere un carrello prima di entrare.
Let's get a shopping cart before going inside.

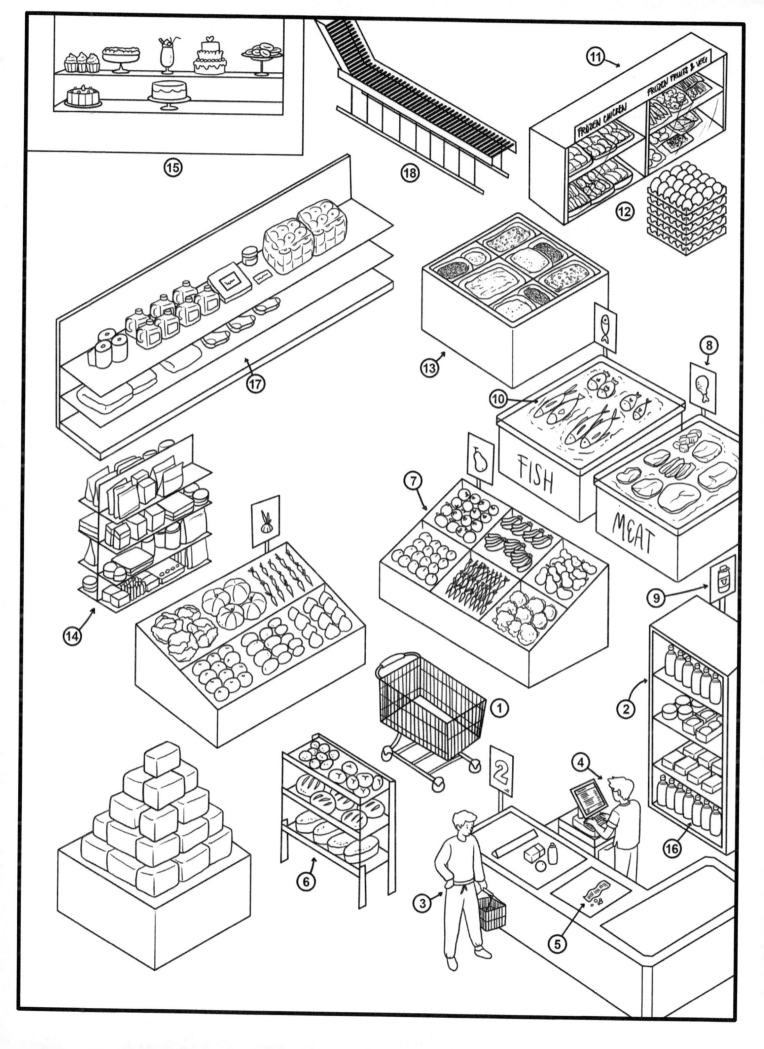

MEDIA (MEDIA)

1) **rivista** (magazine)
   ree-VEE-stah

2) **fax** (fax)
   fahx

3) **giornale** (newspaper)
   jeohr-NAH-leh

4) **posta** (mail)
   POH-stah

5) **lettera** (letter)
   LEHT-teh-rah

6) **radio** (radio)
   RAH-deoh

7) **fumetto** (comic)
   foo-MEHT-toh

8) **libro** (book)
   LEE-broh

9) **fotografia** (photography)
   phoh-toh-grah-PHE-ah

10) **telefono fisso** (landline phone)
    teh-LEH-pho-noh FEE-soh

11) **TV** (TV)
    tee-VOO

12) **film** (movies)
    feelm

13) **cellulare** (mobile phone/cell phone)
    chel-loo-LAH-reh

14) **linguaggio dei segni** (sign language)
    leen-goo-AH-jeoh DEH-ee SEH-ñee

Stasera guarderemo la TV.
Tonight we will watch TV.

Il telefono fisso sta squillando! Puoi rispondere?
The landline phone is ringing! Could you answer?

Sono abbonata a una rivista di moda.
I subscribed to a fashion magazine.

LA FIERA/IL PARCO DIVERTIMENTI (THE FAIR/THE AMUSEMENT PARK)

1) **casa degli specchi** (house of mirrors)
   KAH-sah DEH-llee SPEH-key

2) **nave dei pirati** (pirate ship/boat swing)
   NAH-veh DEH-ee pee-RAH-tee

3) **biglietteria** (ticket booth)
   bee-lleht-teh-REE-ah

4) **altalena** (swing ride)
   ahl-tah-LEH-nah

5) **montagne russe** (roller coaster)
   mohn-TAH-ñeh ROO-seh

6) **ruota panoramica** (Ferris wheel)
   roo-OH-tah pah-noh-RAH-mee-kah

7) **giostra** (carousel/merry-go-round)
   JEOH-strah

8) **autoscontro** (bumper cars)
   AH-oo-toh SKOHN-troh

9) **tazzine** (teacups/cup and saucer)
   tah-DZEE-neh

10) **pendolo** (pendulum)
    PEHN-doh-loh

11) **sala giochi** (arcade)
    SAH-lah JEOH-key

12) **wurstel** (hotdog)
    VEEOO-stehl

13) **cono gelato** (ice cream cone)
    KOH-noh geh-LAH-toh

14) **zucchero filato** (cotton candy)
    DZOO-keh-roh phe-LAH-toh

15) **mela caramellata** (candy apple)
    MEH-lah kah-rah-mehl-LAH-tah

Sei abbastanza coraggioso da andare sulle montagne russe?
Are you brave enough to ride the roller coaster?

Andiamo alla biglietteria per ritirare i nostri biglietti.
Let's go to the ticket booth to pick up our tickets.

Non si è mai troppo vecchi per lo zucchero filato!
You are never too old for cotton candy!

EVENTI DI VITA (LIFE EVENTS)

1) **nascita** (birth)
NAH-she-tah

2) **battesimo** (christening/baptism)
bah-TEH-sea-moh

3) **iniziare la scuola** (start school)
ee-nee-DZEAH-reh lah scoo-OH-lah

4) **farsi degli amici** (make friends)
FAH-rsee DEH-llee ah-MEE-chi

5) **compleanno** (birthday)
kohm-pleh-AHN-noh

6) **innamorarsi** (fall in love)
een-nah-moh-RAHR-sea

7) **laurearsi** (graduate)
lah-oo-reh-AHR-sea

8) **iniziare l'università** (start university/begin college)
ee-nee-DZEAH-reh loo-nee-vehr-sea-TAH

9) **trovare un lavoro** (get a job)
troh-VAH-reh oon lah-VOH-roh

10) **diventare un imprenditore** (become an entrepreneur)
dee-vehn-TAH-reh oon eem-prehn-dee-TOH-reh

11) **viaggiare per il mondo** (travel around the world)
vee-ah-JEAH-reh pehr eel MOHN-doh

12) **sposarsi** (get married)
spoh-SAHR-sea

13) **avere un figlio** (have a baby)
ah-VEH-reh oon FEE-lloh

14) **organizzare feste per bambini** (organize children's parties)
ohr-gah-nee-DZAH-reh FEH-steh pehr bahm-BEE-nee

15) **pensione** (retirement)
pehn-sea-OH-neh

16) **morte** (death)
MOHR-teh

Dovrebbe laurearsi l'anno prossimo.
He/She should graduate next year.

Non vedo l'ora di trovare un lavoro!
I am looking forward to getting a job!

Il nostro sogno è viaggiare per il mondo con uno zaino in spalla.
Our dream is traveling around the world as backpackers.

AGGETTIVI I (ADJECTIVES I)

1) **grande** (big)
GRAHN-deh

2) **piccolo** (small)
PEE-koh-loh

3) **forte** (loud)
FOHR-teh

4) **silenzioso** (silent)
sea-lehn-DZEOH-soh

5) **lungo** (long)
LOON-goh

6) **corto** (short)
KOHR-toh

7) **largo** (wide)
LAHR-goh

8) **stretto** (narrow)
STREHT-toh

9) **costoso** (expensive)
koh-STOH-soh

10) **economico** (cheap)
eh-koh-NOH-mee-koh

11) **veloce** (fast)
veh-LOH-che

12) **lento** (slow)
LEHN-toh

13) **vuoto** (empty)
voo-OH-toh

14) **pieno** (full)
pee-EH-noh

15) **morbido** (soft)
MOHR-bee-doh

16) **duro** (hard)
DOO-roh

17) **alto** (tall)
AHL-toh

18) **basso** (short)
BAHS-soh

Questa borsa è troppo costosa. Non la comprerò.
This bag is too expensive. I will not buy it.

Il loro letto è troppo morbido!
Their bed is too soft!

Suo fratello è altissimo, mentre lei è piuttosto bassa.
Her brother is very tall, while she is quite short.

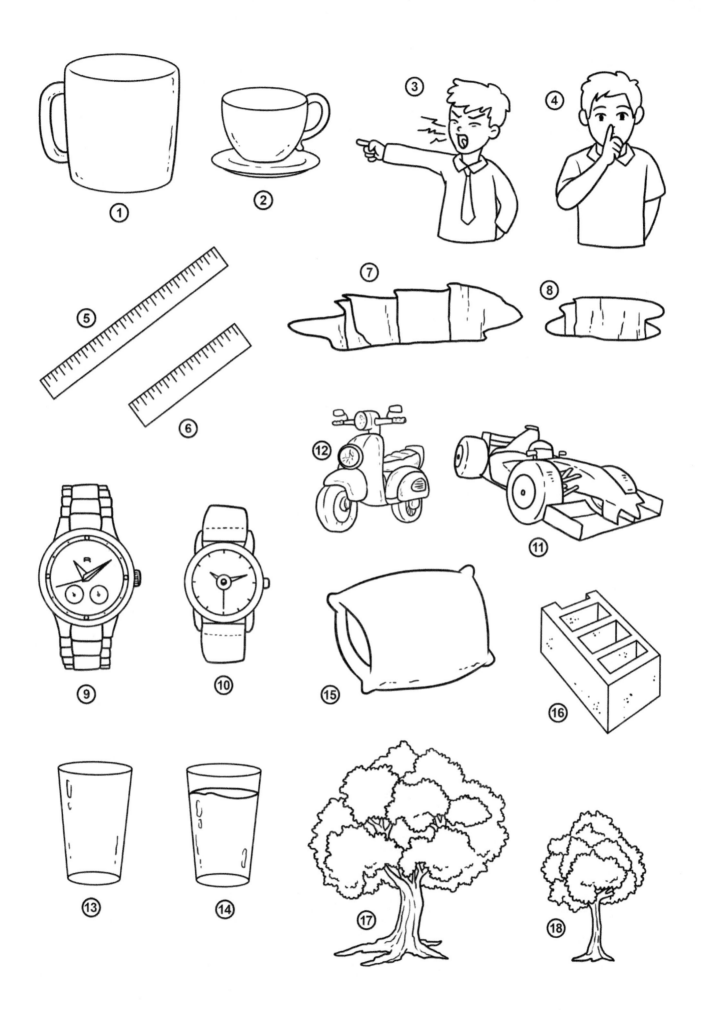

QUIZ #6

Use arrows to match the corresponding translations:

a. circle

b. roller coaster

c. hard

d. magazine

e. honey

f. start school

g. desserts

h. get married

i. birth

j. mustard

k. triangle

l. lobster

m. silent

n. fried chicken

o. expensive

p. receipt

1. triangolo

2. nascita

3. pollo fritto

4. mostarda

5. montagne russe

6. aragosta

7. costoso

8. duro

9. iniziare la scuola

10. scontrino

11. rivista

12. cerchio

13. sposarsi

14. miele

15. dolci

16. silenzioso

Fill in the blank spaces with the options below (use each word only once):

Quando ho aperto il _____, ho visto che era _____. Dovevo assolutamente andare al _____. Ho preso la _____ e, una volta parcheggiato, sono andata a prendere un _____. Mio figlio è allergico ai _____, quindi di solito non li compro. Ho preso molta _____ e degli _____ per la merenda. Mi piace molto il _____, quindi ho comprato dello _____ e un'_____ per cena, anche se non è molto _____.

economica   sgombro

latticini   vuoto

snack   macchina

aragosta   pesce

supermercato   frigorifero

carrello   frutta e verdura

AGGETTIVI II (ADJECTIVES II)

1) **nuovo** (new)
noo-OH-voh

2) **vecchio** (old)
VEH-key-oh

3) **comodo** (comfortable)
KOH-moh-doh

4) **scomodo** (uncomfortable)
SKOH-moh-doh

5) **pericoloso** (dangerous)
peh-ree-koh-LOH-soh

6) **fastidioso** (annoying)
fah-stee-DEOH-soh

7) **instabile** (shaky)
een-STAH-bee-leh

8) **completo** (complete)
kohm-PLEH-toh

9) **incompleto** (incomplete)
een-kohm-PLEH-toh

10) **rotto** (broken)
ROHT-toh

11) **bellissimo** (gorgeous)
behl-LEES-sea-moh

12) **virtuoso** (virtuous)
veer-too-OH-soh

13) **simile** (similar)
SEA-mee-leh

14) **diverso** (different)
dee-VEHR-soh

15) **aperto** (open)
ah-PEHR-toh

16) **chiuso** (closed)
key-OO-soh

Il negozio è chiuso nel fine settimana.
The store is closed on the weekend.

Hai visto la sua macchina nuova?
Did you see his/her new car?

Il supporto del computer è instabile.
The computer stand is shaky.

AVVERBI (ADVERBS)

1) **qui** (here)
coo-EE

2) **là/lì** (there)
lah/lee

3) **vicino** (near)
vee-CHI-noh

4) **lontano** (far)
lohn-TAH-noh

5) **sopra** (above)
SOH-prah

6) **sotto** (below)
SOHT-toh

7) **dentro** (inside)
DEHN-troh

8) **fuori** (outside)
foo-OH-ree

9) **davanti** (ahead)
dah-VAHN-tee

10) **dietro** (behind)
dee-EH-troh

11) **no** (no)
noh

12) **sì** (yes)
see

13) **adesso/ora** (now)
ah-DEHS-soh/OH-rah

14) **bene/giusto** (well/good/right)
BEH-neh/jee-OO-stoh

15) **male/sbagliato** (bad/wrong)
MAH-leh/sbah-llee-AH-toh

Adesso viviamo a Londra, ma ci siamo trasferiti da poco.
We now live in London, but we just moved in.

La stazione non è così lontana.
The train station is not that far.

Vieni qui!
Come here!

148

DIREZIONI (DIRECTIONS)

1) **isolato** (block)
   ee-soh-LAH-toh

2) **piazza** (square)
   pee-AH-dzah

3) **parco** (park)
   PAHR-koh

4) **metro** (subway)
   MEH-troh

5) **angolo** (corner)
   AHN-goh-loh

6) **viale** (avenue)
   vee-AH-leh

7) **strada/via** (street)
   STRAH-dah/VEE-ah

8) **fermata del bus** (bus stop)
   fehr-MAH-tah dehl boos

9) **semaforo** (traffic light)
   seh-MAH-phoh-roh

10) **strisce pedonali** (crossing/crosswalk)
    STREE-sche peh-doh-NAH-lee

11) **su** (up)
    soo

12) **giù** (down)
    jeoo

13) **sinistra** (left)
    see-NEE-strah

14) **destra** (right)
    DEH-strah

15) **cartelli stradali** (road signs)
    kahr-TEHL-lee strah-DAH-lee

16) **vigile urbano** (traffic police)
    VEE-jee-leh oor-BAH-noh

La banca è a sinistra, accanto alla piazza.
The bank is on the left, next to the square.

Per attraversare la strada dobbiamo aspettare il verde.
To cross the street, we need to wait for the green light.

Il parco è bellissimo! Dovremmo andarci insieme.
The park is gorgeous! We should go there together.

IL RISTORANTE (THE RESTAURANT)

1) **manager** (manager)
MAH-nah-gehr

2) **tavolo** (table)
TAH-voh-loh

3) **menù** (menu)
meh-NOO

4) **piatto** (dish)
pee-AHT-toh

5) **stuzzichini** (appetizers)
stoo-dzee-KEY-nee

6) **antipasto** (starter)
ahn-tee-PAH-stoh

7) **piatto principale** (main course)
pee-AHT-toh preen-chi-PAH-leh

8) **dolce** (dessert)
DOHL-che

9) **tavola calda** (diner)
TAH-voh-lah KAHL-dah

10) **cuoco** (cook)
coo-OH-koh

11) **cameriere** (waiter)
kah-meh-ree-EH-reh

12) **cameriera** (waitress)
kah-meh-ree-EH-rah

13) **mancia** (tip)
MAHN-chi-ah

14) **seggiolone** (high chair)
seh-jeoh-LOH-neh

15) **lista dei vini** (wine list)
LEE-stah DEH-ee VEE-nee

16) **pasticcere** (pastry chef)
pah-stee-CHE-reh

Non prendo l'antipasto anche se ho molta fame.
I will not have a starter, even if I am very hungry.

La mancia non è obbligatoria in Italia, ma è sempre la benvenuta!
Tips are not mandatory in Italy, but they are always welcome!

Possiamo fare i complimenti al cuoco?
Can we compliment the cook?

IL CENTRO COMMERCIALE (THE MALL)

1) **piano** (floor)
pee-AH-noh

2) **acquario** (aquarium)
ah-coo-AH-reeoh

3) **area ristoro** (food court)
AH-reh-ah ree-STOH-roh

4) **ascensore** (elevator)
ah-schen-SOH-reh

5) **scale mobili** (escalators)
SKAH-leh MOH-bee-lee

6) **uscita di emergenza** (emergency exit)
oo-SHE-tah dee eh-mehr-GEHN-dzah

7) **salone di bellezza** (beauty salon)
sah-LOH-neh dee behl-LEH-dzah

8) **negozio di abbigliamento** (clothing store)
neh-GOH-dzeeoh dee ah-bee-llah-MEHN-toh

9) **area giochi** (playground)
AH-reah JEOH-kih

10) **guardia giurata** (security guard)
goo-AHR-deeah jeoo-RAH-tah

11) **videocamera di sorveglianza** (surveillance camera)
vee-deh-oh-KAH-meh-rah dee sohr-veh-LLAHN-dzah

12) **forno** (bakery)
FOHR-noh

13) **negozio sportivo** (sports store)
neh-GOH-dzeoh spohr-TEE-voh

14) **fontana** (fountain)
fohn-TAH-nah

Incontriamoci alla fontana alle 3.
Let's meet at the fountain at 3.

Prendo le scale mobili. Ho paura degli ascensori!
I will take the escalators. I am scared of elevators!

Il salone di bellezza è al secondo piano.
The beauty salon is on the second floor.

VERBI I (VERBS I)

1) **parlare** (to talk)
   pahr-LAH-reh

2) **bere** (to drink)
   BEH-reh

3) **mangiare** (to eat)
   mahn-JEAH-reh

4) **camminare** (to walk)
   kahm-mee-NAH-reh

5) **aprire** (to open)
   ah-PREE-reh

6) **chiudere** (to close)
   key-OO-deh-reh

7) **dare** (to give)
   DAH-reh

8) **vedere** (to see)
   veh-DEH-reh

9) **seguire** (to follow)
   seh-goo-EE-reh

10) **abbracciare** (to hug)
    ahb-brah-chi-AH-reh

11) **baciare** (to kiss)
    bah-chi-AH-reh

12) **comprare** (to buy)
    kohm-PRAH-reh

13) **ascoltare** (to listen)
    ah-skohl-TAH-reh

14) **cantare** (to sing)
    kahn-TAH-reh

15) **ballare** (to dance)
    bahl-LAH-reh

Mi piacerebbe cantare, ma sono stonato come una campana.
I would like to sing, but I cannot carry a tune.

Lascia che ti abbracci!
Let me hug you!

Per favore, chiudi la porta quando esci.
Close the door when you go out, please.

VERBI II (VERBS II)

1) **scrivere** (to write)
SKREE-veh-reh

2) **leggere** (to read)
LEH-geh-reh

3) **pulire** (to clean)
poo-LEE-reh

4) **raccogliere** (to pick up)
rah-KOH-lleh-reh

5) **trovare** (to find)
troh-VAH-reh

6) **lavare** (to wash)
lah-VAH-reh

7) **guardare** (to watch)
goo-ahr-DAH-reh

8) **riparare** (to fix)
ree-pah-RAH-reh

9) **pensare** (to think)
pehn-SAH-reh

10) **prendere** (to take)
PREHN-deh-reh

11) **tagliare** (to cut)
tah-LLAH-reh

12) **fermare** (to stop)
fehr-MAH-reh

13) **piangere** (to cry)
pee-AHN-geh-reh

14) **sorridere** (to smile)
sohr-REE-deh-reh

15) **aiutare** (to help)
ah-ee-oo-TAH-reh

Sai riparare una bicicletta?
Are you able to fix a bike?

Questo fine settimana devi pulire la tua camera. Niente scuse!
This weekend, you must clean your room. No excuses!

Ho scritto una cartolina per i miei nonni.
I wrote a postcard for my grandparents.

COSTRUZIONI I (CONSTRUCTION I)

1) **gru** (crane)
groo

2) **nastro di pericolo** (hazard tape)
NAH-stroh dee peh-REE-koh-loh

3) **cono stradale** (traffic cone)
KOH-noh strah-DAH-leh

4) **pala da costruzioni** (construction shovel)
PAH-lah dah koh-stroo-DZEOH-nee

5) **martello** (hammer)
mahr-TEHL-loh

6) **tronchese** (wire cutters)
trohn-KEH-seh

7) **rullo di vernice** (paint roller)
ROOL-loh dee vehr-NEE-che

8) **motosega** (chainsaw)
moh-toh-SEH-gah

9) **trapano** (drill)
TRAH-pah-noh

10) **martello pneumatico** (jackhammer)
mahr-TEHL-loh pneh-oo-MAH-tee-koh

11) **pinze** (pliers)
PEEN-dzeh

12) **cacciavite** (screwdriver)
kah-chi-ah-VEE-teh

Mi puoi prestare il tuo martello?
Could you lend me your hammer?

Fai attenzione ai coni stradali mentre guidi.
Pay attention to the traffic cones while driving.

Ho perso il cacciavite. Vado a comprarne uno nuovo.
I have lost my screwdriver. I will go buy a new one.

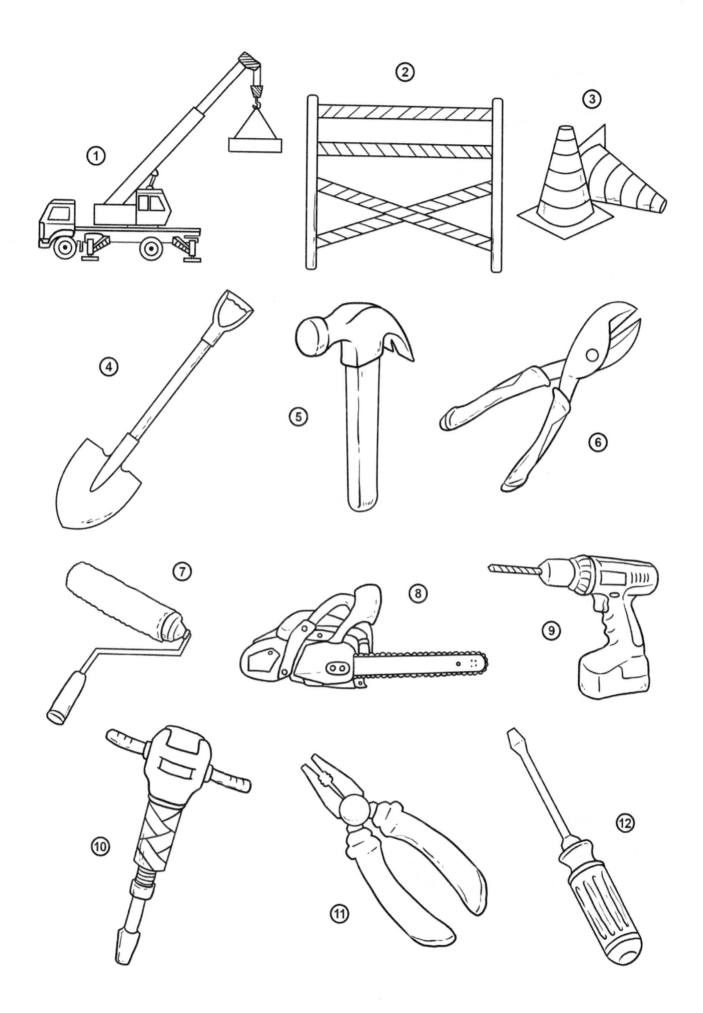

COSTRUZIONI II (CONSTRUCTION II)

1) **cassetta degli attrezzi** (toolbox)
   kahs-SEHT-tah DEH-llee aht-TREH-dzee

2) **caschetto** (work helmet/hard hat)
   kah-SKEHT-toh

3) **progetto** (blueprint)
   proh-JET-toh

4) **tubi** (pipes)
   TOO-bee

5) **cazzuola** (trowel)
   kah-dzoo-OH-lah

6) **betoniera** (concrete mixer)
   beh-toh-nee-EH-rah

7) **mattone** (brick)
   maht-TOH-neh

8) **materiali da costruzione** (building materials)
   mah-teh-ree-AH-lee dah koh-stroo-DZEOH-neh

9) **piastrelle** (tiles)
   pee-ah-STREHL-leh

10) **cemento** (cement)
    che-MEHN-toh

11) **sabbia** (sand)
    SAH-bee-ah

12) **ghiaia** (gravel)
    ghee-AH-ee-ah

Ho comprato delle nuove piastrelle per il bagno.
I bought new tiles for the bathroom.

Hai letto il progetto?
Did you read the blueprint?

Non dimenticare di indossare il caschetto.
Do not forget to wear the work helmet.

QUIZ #7

Use arrows to match the corresponding translations:

a. to take

b. elevator

c. there

d. to dance

e. toolbox

f. avenue

g. left

h. to kiss

i. waitress

j. street

k. right

l. building materials

m. tip

n. traffic lights

o. to drink

p. to clean

1. cassetta degli attrezzi

2. destra

3. materiali da costruzione

4. lì

5. mancia

6. semaforo

7. sinistra

8. ascensore

9. bere

10. viale

11. pulire

12. via

13. ballare

14. prendere

15. cameriera

16. baciare

Fill in the blank spaces with the options below (use each word only once):

Benvenuti nella mia _____ città! Non c'è molto da _____, ma per me è perfetto. Non mi piacciono le città _____. Una volta arrivati, se girate a _____, c'è casa mia. Per andare al _____ preferisco _____, non ho bisogno di _____ la macchina perché ci vogliono solo cinque minuti. Il mio _____ preferito è lungo il _____, i _____ sono gentilissimi e il _____ è fenomenale! C'è anche un grande _____ dove vado spesso il fine settimana.

ristorante

cuoco

piccola

camerieri

vedere

supermercato

prendere

centro commerciale

grandi

viale

camminare

destra

PIANTE E ALBERI (PLANTS AND TREES)

1) **fiori selvatici** (wildflowers)
fee-OH-ree sehl-VAH-tee-chi

2) **erba aromatica** (herb)
EHR-bah ah-roh-MAH-tee-kah

3) **funghi** (mushrooms)
PHOON-ghee

4) **erbaccia** (weed)
ehr-BAH-chi-ah

5) **alga** (seaweed)
AHL-gah

6) **felce** (fern)
PHEL-che

7) **canna** (reed)
KAHN-nah

8) **bambù** (bamboo)
bahm-BOO

9) **edera** (ivy)
EH-deh-rah

10) **muschio** (moss)
MOO-ski-oh

11) **erba** (grass)
EHR-bah

12) **palma** (palm tree)
PAHL-mah

13) **mangrovia** (mangrove)
mahn-GROH-vee-ah

14) **cactus** (cactus)
KAH-ktoos

I colori dei fiori selvatici sono bellissimi.
The colors of wildflowers are stunning.

Per trovare il nord, segui il muschio!
To find north, follow the moss!

Sai riconoscere i diversi tipi di funghi?
Can you recognize the different types of mushrooms?

IL CARNEVALE (THE CARNIVAL)

1) **maschera** (mask)
MAH-skeh-rah

2) **costume/travestimento**
(costume/disguise)
koh-STOO-meh/trah-veh-stee-MEHN-toh

3) **carro** (float)
KAHR-roh

4) **fiori** (flowers)
fee-OH-ree

5) **tamburo** (snare drum)
tahm-BOO-roh

6) **pagliaccio/clown** (clown)
pah-LLAH-chi-oh/clown

7) **supereroe** (superhero)
soo-pehr-eh-ROH-eh

8) **principessa** (princess)
preen-chi-PEHS-sah

9) **astronauta** (astronaut)
ah-stroh-NAH-oo-tah

10) **mimo** (mime)
MEE-moh

11) **prigioniero** (prisoner)
pree-jeo-nee-EH-roh

12) **elettrodomestico** (household appliance)
eh-leht-troh-doh-MEH-stee-koh

13) **fatina** (fairy)
fah-TEE-nah

14) **boscaiolo** (lumberjack)
boh-skah-ee-OH-loh

I pagliacci mi fanno paura da morire!
Clowns scare me to death!

Indosserai un costume per il prossimo Carnevale?
Will you wear a costume for next Carnival?

Che cosa mi serve per travestirmi da boscaiolo?
What do I need to dress up as a lumberjack?

L'OFFICINA (THE WORKSHOP)

1) **attrezzo/strumento** (tool)
   aht-TREH-dzoh/stroo-MEHN-toh

2) **selleria** (saddlery)
   sehl-leh-REE-ah

3) **falegnameria**
   (carpentry/woodworking)
   fah-leh-ñah-meh-REE-ah

4) **tappezzeria** (upholstery/tapestry)
   tahp-peh-dzeh-REE-ah

5) **calzoleria** (shoemaking/shoe repair)
   kahl-dzoh-leh-REE-ah

6) **orafo** (silversmith)
   OH-rah-pho

7) **fabbro** (blacksmith)
   PHA-broh

8) **meccanico** (mechanic)
   meh-KAH-nee-koh

9) **tessile** (textile)
   TEH-sea-leh

10) **forno** (bakery)
    PHOR-noh

11) **bigiotteria** (costume jewelry)
    bee-jeoht-teh-REE-ah

12) **calzature** (footwear)
    kahl-dzah-TOO-reh

13) **manutenzione** (maintenance)
    mah-noo-tehn-DZEOH-neh

14) **riparazione** (repair)
    ree-pah-rah-DZEOH-neh

15) **pittura** (painting)
    peet-TOO-rah

16) **pasticceria** (pastry shop)
    pah-stee-che-REE-ah

La mia auto è rotta. Mi serve un meccanico.
My car broke. I need a mechanic.

Hanno comprato tutti i mobili in una falegnameria.
They bought all their furniture at a woodworking shop.

Il suo sogno? Lavorare in una pasticceria e mangiare gratis!
His/Her dream? Working in a pastry shop and eating for free!

IL NEGOZIO DI ALIMENTARI (THE GROCERY STORE)

1) **pasta** (pasta)
PAH-stah

2) **riso** (rice)
REE-soh

3) **avena** (oat)
ah-VEH-nah

4) **pane** (bread)
PAH-neh

5) **oli** (oils)
OH-lee

6) **salse** (sauces)
SAHL-seh

7) **condimenti per insalate** (salad dressings)
kohn-dee-MEHN-tee pehr een-sah-LAH-teh

8) **condimenti** (condiments)
kohn-dee-MEHN-tee

9) **cibi in scatola** (canned goods)
CHI-bee een SKAH-toh-lah

10) **prosciutto** (ham)
proh-she-OO-toh

11) **formaggio** (cheese)
phor-MAH-jeoh

12) **burro di arachidi** (peanut butter)
BOO-roh dee ah-RAH-kih-dee

13) **dolciumi** (candy)
dohl-chi-OO-mee

14) **fagioli** (beans)
pha-JEOH-lee

15) **caffè** (coffee)
kah-PHEH

16) **tè** (tea)
tèh

Per iniziare la giornata prendo sempre un buon caffè.
To start the day, I always have a good coffee.

Un panino con prosciutto e formaggio, per favore.
A sandwich with ham and cheese, please.

Preferisci il riso o la pasta per pranzo?
Do you prefer rice or pasta for lunch?

VIAGGI E VITA I (TRAVEL AND LIVING I)

1) **guida** (guide)
goo-EE-dah

2) **turista** (tourist)
too-REE-stah

3) **viaggiatore** (traveler)
vee-ah-jeah-TOH-reh

4) **valigia** (luggage)
vah-LEE-jeah

5) **bagaglio a mano** (hand luggage)
bah-GAH-lleoh ah MAH-noh

6) **macchina fotografica** (camera)
MAH-kih-nah pho-toh-GRAH-phee-kah

7) **hotel** (hotel)
oh-TEHL

8) **ostello** (hostel)
oh-STEHL-loh

9) **Bed and Breakfast** (bed & breakfast/inn)
behd ehnd BREHK-fast

10) **bungalow** (cabin)
BOON-gah-loh

11) **tenda** (tent)
TEHN-dah

12) **volo** (flight)
VOH-loh

13) **partenza** (departure)
pahr-TEHN-dzah

14) **arrivo** (arrival)
ahr-REE-voh

Ho dimenticato la macchina fotografica in hotel.
I forgot the camera in the hotel.

Viaggiamo solo con il bagaglio a mano.
We travel with hand luggage only.

A che ora è prevista la vostra partenza?
What time is your expected departure?

VIAGGI E VITA II (TRAVEL AND LIVING II)

1) **città** (town)
chi-TAH

2) **piantina** (map)
pee-ahn-TEE-nah

3) **fermata del bus** (bus stop)
pher-MAH-tah dehl boos

4) **taxi** (taxi)
TAH-xee

5) **noleggio auto** (car rental)
noh-LEH-jeoh AH-oo-toh

6) **stazione** (train station)
stah-DZEOH-neh

7) **aeroporto** (airport)
ah-eh-roh-POHR-toh

8) **passaporto** (passport)
pahs-sah-POHR-toh

9) **carta di identità** (ID/identification card)
KAHR-tah dee-dehn-tee-TAH

10) **valuta** (currency)
vah-LOO-tah

11) **contanti** (cash)
kohn-TAHN-tee

12) **carta di debito** (debit card)
KAHR-tah dee DEH-bee-toh

13) **carta di credito** (credit card)
KAHR-tah dee KREH-dee-toh

14) **guida turistica** (tourist guide)
goo-EE-dah too-REE-stee-kah

Mi scusi, mi sa dire dov'è la stazione?
Excuse me, could you tell me where the station is?

Possiamo pagare con carta di credito?
Can we pay by credit card?

Devono essere in aeroporto per le 5.
They have to be at the airport by 5.

GIOCATTOLI (TOYS)

1) **pallone/palla** (ball)
   pahl-LOH-neh/PAHL-lah

2) **orsetto** (teddy bear)
   ohr-SEH-toh

3) **trenino** (train)
   treh-NEE-noh

4) **skateboard** (skateboard)
   as in English

5) **bambola** (doll)
   BAHM-boh-lah

6) **macchinina da corsa** (toy racing car)
   mah-kih-NEE-nah dah KOHR-sah

7) **robot** (robot)
   ROH-boh

8) **aquilone** (kite)
   ah-coo-ee-LOH-neh

9) **tamburo** (drum)
   tahm-BOO-roh

10) **hula hoop** (hula hoop)
    OO-lah ohp

11) **camion** (wagon)
    KAH-mee-ohn

12) **mattoncini** (blocks)
    maht-tohn-CHI-nee

13) **xilofono** (xylophone)
    xee-LOH-phoh-noh

14) **furgoncino** (truck)
    phoor-gohn-CHI-noh

15) **aeroplanino** (airplane)
    ah-eh-roh-plah-NEE-noh

16) **costruzioni** (bricks)
    koh-stroo-DZEOH-nee

Non lascia mai il suo orsetto!
He/She never leaves his/her teddy bear!

Oggi è ventoso! Prendiamo l'acquilone?
Today it is windy! Shall we take the kite?

Ai miei figli piace molto giocare con il tamburo, ma che casino!
My children really like playing with the drum, but what a racket!

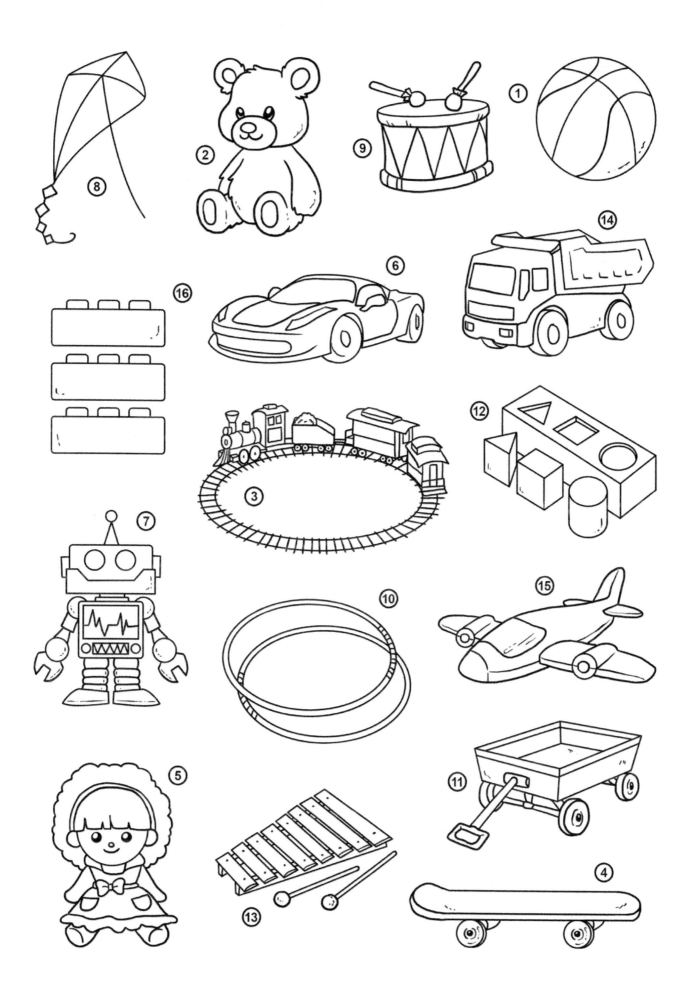

LA FESTA DI COMPLEANNO (THE BIRTHDAY PARTY)

1) **striscione di compleanno** (birthday banner)
stree-sche-OH-neh dee kohm-pleh-AHN-noh

2) **decorazioni** (decorations)
deh-koh-rah-DZEOH-nee

3) **regalo** (present/gift)
reh-GAH-loh

4) **servizio da tavola** (tableware)
sehr-VEE-dzeoh dah TAH-voh-lah

5) **festeggiato** (birthday person)
phe-steh-JEAH-toh

6) **palloncino** (balloon)
pahl-lohn-CHI-noh

7) **torta di compleanno** (birthday cake)
TOHR-tah dee kohm-pleh-AHN-noh

8) **piattini** (plates)
pee-aht-TEE-nee

9) **forchette** (forks)
phor-KEHT-teh

10) **cucchiai** (spoons)
coo-kih-AH-ee

11) **bicchieri** (cups)
bee-kih-EH-ree

12) **cannuccia** (straw)
kahn-NOO-chi-ah

13) **pentolaccia** (piñata)
pehn-toh-LAH-chi-ah

14) **candeline** (candles)
kahn-deh-LEE-neh

15) **cappellino** (hat)
kahp-peh-LEE-noh

16) **invitati** (guests)
een-vee-TAH-tee

Quanti invitati ci sono alla festa?
How many guests are there at the party?

Sulla torta ci sono ventisette candeline.
There are twenty-seven candles on the cake.

Non dimentichiamo di mettere i piattini sul tavolo.
Let's not forget to put the plates on the table.

CONTRARI (OPPOSITES)

1) **pulito** (clean)
   poo-LEE-toh

2) **sporco** (dirty)
   SPOHR-koh

3) **pochi** (few)
   POH-kih

4) **molti** (many)
   MOHL-tee

5) **attacco** (attack)
   aht-TAH-koh

6) **difesa** (defense)
   dee-PHEH-sah

7) **dritto** (straight)
   DREE-toh

8) **curvo** (curved)
   COOR-voh

9) **insieme** (together)
   een-sea-EH-meh

10) **separati** (separated)
    seh-pah-RAH-tee

11) **giovane** (young)
    JEOH-vah-neh

12) **vecchio** (old)
    VEH-kih-oh

13) **abbondante** (plentiful)
    ahb-bohn-DAHN-teh

14) **carente** (scarce)
    kah-REHN-teh

15) **concavo** (concave)
    KOHN-kah-voh

16) **convesso** (convex)
    kohn-VEH-soh

Meglio pochi ma buoni!
Better fewer, but better!

Il mio capo è piuttosto giovane, ma ha molta esperienza.
My boss is quite young, but has much experience.

Paghiamo il conto insieme.
Let's pay the bill together.

QUIZ #8

Use arrows to match the corresponding translations:

a. guests

b. mask

c. grass

d. tool

e. teddy bear

f. tent

g. camera

h. fairy

i. candle

j. rice

k. old

l. mushroom

m. birthday person

n. train (toy)

o. ID

p. straw

1. orsetto

2. candelina

3. funghi

4. erba

5. cannuccia

6. vecchio

7. strumento

8. riso

9. carta di identità

10. festeggiato

11. macchina fotografica

12. fatina

13. tenda

14. maschera

15. trenino

16. invitati

Fill in the blank spaces with the options below (use each word only once):

Ieri era il mio _____ ! Per festeggiare, ho organizzato una _____ con una trentina di _____, i miei più cari amici. Sì, eravamo _____, ma è stato molto divertente. Ho ricevuto diversi _____, tra cui una bellissima _____ e un buono per un _____ in _____, e alla fine ho soffiato le _____ sulla mia _____. C'erano amici _____, conosciuti da poco, e _____, che conosco da una vita.

nuovi

molti

macchina fotografica

aereo

invitati

regali

candeline

vecchi

festa

compleanno

torta

viaggio

CONCLUSION

Obviously, there are still many things to say about the Italian language, and tons of new words to learn, but we really hope that this general overview will help you during this journey into Italian.

This is just the first step—now it is your turn!

Before ending this dicitionary book, we would like to leave you with a few suggestions for a pleasant and fruitful language learning experience:

1. Be motivated. If you do not enjoy what you are learning, this journey will not make sense anymore. Enjoy the challenges of the language, play with the vocabulary you learn on a daily basis, and do not forget to celebrate your accomplishments!

2. Write your own vocabulary list. We know, writing can be annoying and requires much time. However, having your own list of words—even better if you create different ones for nouns, adjectives, adverbs and verbs—will come in handy. *Fidati!* Trust us!

3. Use all the resources that you can find in order to improve your knowledge. Movies, podcasts, songs, TV series, everything is useful! If you would like to watch an Italian movie/TV series, our advice is to watch it with English subtitles first. Then, as soon as you feel confident enough, put the subtitles in Italian. It does not matter if you do not understand every single word. What really matters is understanding the meaning of the sentence, and you will also see that you will learn new words in a fast and fun way!

4. Do not be afraid of speaking in Italian with the locals. As soon as you have the chance, please talk to them! We understand that you might be scared of making mistakes or saying something wrong, but you will see that all these fears live in your head only. Italian people are very friendly, and will definitely appreciate your effort! *Coraggio!* Go for it!

5. Remember that learning a new language requires much practice. Do not feel disappointed if you feel that you are still struggling with Italian. It is perfectly normal!

6. Do not forget to have fun!

ANSWERS

QUIZ #1

a-5   b-11   c-8   d-15   e-4   f-16   g-13   h-1   i-6   j-14   k-2   l-7   m-9
n12   o-3   p-10

Francesco stava giocando a calcio con il suo **cane**, quando suo **fratello** lo ha chiamato per dirgli di tornare a casa. Suo fratello, Carlo, sembrava molto **preoccupato** al telefono. Dopo poco lo chiamano anche i **nonni**. Francesco, che è un ragazzo **ansioso**, prende subito il pallone e torna a casa, dove trova sua **sorella** Lidia con la **mano** sul **piede**. Era caduta dalle scale! Arrivano all'ospedale e, per fortuna, non era niente di grave. Lidia, infatti, non aveva battuto la **testa** durante la caduta. I medici le hanno detto che deve solo riposare! Adesso è sul divano a guardare un documentario sugli **animali** con il suo **gatto** persiano e sua **madre**.

QUIZ #2

a-4   b-10   c-1   d-9   e-7   f-5   g-2   h-13   i-3   j-16   k-15   l-6   m-14
n-11   o-8   p-12

La mia stagione preferita è **l'estate**. Fa **caldo,** il **freddo** dell'inverno è solo un brutto ricordo, e posso andare in **piscina** con i miei amici per **nuotare** la mattina o il pomeriggio. Un'altra cosa che mi piace fare in compagnia sono i **picnic** al **parco**. Ognuno porta qualcosa di diverso da mangiare. Adoro andare al mare e vedere gli animali marini. Una volta ho persino visto dei **delfini** che saltavano tra le onde! Gli animali che non vorrei vedere, però, sono lo **squalo** e la **murena**. Ho troppa paura! La mia cosa preferita da bere è la **limonata** o un bicchiere di acqua ghiacciata, e da mangiare amo i frutti di mare come le **vongole.**

QUIZ #3

a-4   b-14   c-12   d-8   e-16   f-7   g-9   h-1   i-13   j-10   k-15   l-2   m-5

n-3   o-6   p-11

Benvenuti a casa mia! Non è grande, ma è molto accogliente. Al piano terra c'è la mia stanza preferita, il **salotto,** dove ho la **televisione** e la **console** che uso per giocare ai miei videogiochi preferiti. Accanto c'è la **cucina,** dove i miei genitori preparano dei piatti ottimi. La **sala da pranzo** è sulla destra; abbiamo un grande **tavolo da pranzo** che usiamo per mangiare, con una **tovaglia** rossa e un **vaso** con dei fiori bellissimi. Abbiamo sei **sedie,** ma possiamo aggiungerne altre quando abbiamo ospiti. La mia **camera da letto** è al piano di sopra. Il mio **letto** è molto comodo; visto che è inverno, ho le **lenzuola** più pesanti.

QUIZ #4

a-12   b-7   c-13   d-9   e-16   f-3   g-15   h-2   i-6   j-1   k-4   l-5   m-14

n-10   o-8   p-11

Lavoro come **insegnante** in una **scuola** media. Adoro la mia **professione** perché mi permette di condividere le cose che so con i miei **studenti.** Adesso è **Natale,** quindi non c'è scuola e i ragazzi sono in vacanza. Dobbiamo ancora comprare tutti i **regali** e le **candele** per la tavola!

Nel mio tempo libero, mi piace giocare a **pallavolo** e a **pallacanestro** Anche i miei figli fanno sport; loro fanno **boxe** due volte alla settimana. Visto che adesso sono liberi, mi aiutano a mettere le **decorazioni natalizie** in tutta la casa e a preparare gli **omini di zenzero.**

QUIZ #5

a-3   b-8   c-12   d-15   e-1   f-16   g-2   h-10   i-14   j-9   k-6   l-4   m-11

n-5   o-7   p-13

Cosa mi piace fare nel mio tempo libero? Tantissime cose! Suono il **piano** da quando avevo sei anni, e l'**arpa** da un paio di anni. Lavoro come **scienziato,** quindi non ho molto tempo, ma cerco sempre di **suonare** almeno due volte alla settimana. Per lavoro viaggio molto; il mese scorso ero in Argentina, in **America del Sud,** e la prossima settimana dovrò andare in **Asia,** in Cina. Un'altra cosa che mi piace fare è mangiare! Amo la **verdura,** in particolare le **melanzane** e i **cetrioli,** ma sono allergico alle **cipolle.** Per quanto riguarda la frutta, la mia preferita sono le **ciliegie,** ma non mi piace il **melone.**

QUIZ #6

a-12   b-5   c-8   d-11   e-14   f-9   g-15   h-13   i-2   j-4   k-1   l-6   m-16

n-3   o-7   p-10

Quando ho aperto il **frigorifero,** ho visto che era **vuoto.** Dovevo assolutamente andare al **supermercato.** Ho preso la **macchina** e, una volta parcheggiato, sono andata a prendere un **carrello.** Mio figlio è allergico ai **latticini,** quindi di solito non li compro. Ho preso molta **frutta e verdura** e degli **snack** per la merenda. Mi piace molto il **pesce,** quindi ho comprato dello **sgombro** e un'**aragosta** per cena, anche se non è molto **economica.**

QUIZ #7

a-14 b-8 c-4 d-13 e-1 f-10 g-7 h-16 i-15 j-12 k-2 l-3 m-5

n-6 o-9 p-11

Benvenuti nella mia **piccola** città! Non c'è molto da **vedere**, ma per me è perfetto. Non mi piacciono le città **grandi.** Una volta arrivati, se girate a **destra,** c'è casa mia. Per andare al **supermercato** preferisco **camminare,** non ho bisogno di **prendere** la macchina perché ci vogliono solo cinque minuti. Il mio **ristorante** preferito è lungo il **viale,** i **camerieri** sono gentilissimi e il **cuoco** è fenomenale! C'è anche un grande **centro commerciale** dove vado spesso il fine settimana.

QUIZ #8

a-16 b-14 c-4 d-7 e-1 f-13 g-11 h-12 i-2 j-8 k-6 l-3 m-10

n-15 o-9 p-5

Ieri era il mio **compleanno**! Per festeggiare, ho organizzato una **festa** con una trentina di **invitati,** i miei più cari amici. Sì, eravamo **molti,** ma è stato molto divertente. Ho ricevuto diversi **regali,** tra cui una bellissima **macchina fotografica** e un buono per un **viaggio** in **aereo,** e alla fine ho soffiato le **candeline** sulla mia **torta.** C'erano amici **nuovi,** conosciuti da poco, e **vecchi,** che conosco da una vita.

Printed in Great Britain
by Amazon

36922279R00110